COMPLETELY

COMPLETELY

Learning to Abide

VJ Goodman

COMPLETELY Learning to Abide

Copyright © 2023 by Valerie J Goodman
Printed in the United States of America
Published By: Valerie J Goodman goodmanvaleriejean@gmail.com

This work is a blend of Christian non-fiction and personal memoirs; a collection of the author's best recollections. The events and conversations within these pages are drawn from the author's personal life experiences and beliefs. They have been accurately set down to the best of the author's ability.

All rights reserved. No part of this book may be reproduced or used in any manner without written permission of the copyright owner, except for the use of quotations and content for the purpose of ministry. For more information, please contact Valerie J Goodman at goodmanvaleriejean@gmail.com.

Book design and formatting by Valerie J Goodman and A.C. Neal

Cover photography by Crystal Oliver

ISBN: 9798987841907

Scriptures marked MSG are taken from The Message, copyright © 1993, 2002, 2018 by Eugene H. Peterson.

Scriptures marked Holman Christian Standard Bible (HCSB) are taken from Holman Christian Standard Bible, Copyright © 1999, 2000, 2002, 2003, 2009 by Holman Bible Publishers, Nashville Tennessee. All rights reserved.

Scriptures marked NLT are taken from Holy Bible, New Living Translation, copyright © 1996, 2004, 2015 by Tyndale House Foundation. Used by permission of Tyndale House Publishers, Inc., Carol Stream, Illinois 60188. All rights reserved.

Scriptures marked NIV are taken from New International Version NIV, Holy Bible, New International Version®, NIV® Copyright ©1973, 1978, 1984, 2011 by Biblica, Inc.® Used by permission. All rights reserved worldwide.

Scriptures marked NCB are taken from Copyright © 2019 by Catholic Book Publishing Corp. All rights reserved.

Scriptures marked ESV are taken from The English Standard Version, The Holy Bible, English Standard Version. ESV® Text Edition: 2016. Copyright © 2001 by Crossway Bibles, a publishing ministry of Good News Publishers.

Scriptures marked NASB are taken from New American Standard Bible®, Copyright © 1960, 1971, 1977, 1995, 2020 by The Lockman Foundation. All rights reserved.

Scriptures marked MEV are taken from The Holy Bible, Modern English Version. Copyright © 2014 by Military Bible Association. Published and distributed by Charisma House.

Scriptures marked AMP are taken from Copyright © 2015 by The Lockman Foundation, La Habra, CA 90631. All rights reserved.

"**COMPLETELY** encouraged me greatly to trust the Lord in all things and in all trials and tribulations. I laughed out loud and I wept while reading it. You will devour this beautiful, authentic book." —

Sunshine Williamson, Jacksonville State University

DEDICATION

To my God who never gave up on me - together we are flipping the script. May You always receive the Glory and may my story be a survival guide that always points others to Your story.

To Tommy – you have supported my dream and believed in me every step of the way. You have celebrated each leg of the journey and shared in my frustrations. Life with you is the most beautiful place within my heart. Thank you for being my biggest fan! The freedom you have given me to chase after my dream has been the greatest display of love one could give. I love you!

To my family – I am incredibly and eternally grateful to God for the gift you are to me.

To my dear friend - Sunshine Williamson – I prayed for you for years, before I even knew you. May God's richest blessings rest upon you and your family always. Thank you for always believing in me and walking this journey with me. Thank you for giving insight and wisdom - your encouragement has been light.

To Jolene Williamson and Carolyn Smith – I want to thank you both for joining me on this inaugural journey. Your kindness has been refreshing and empowering.

To Andi Neal – you are the gift I never knew I needed. God brought you into my life for such a time as this. Thank you for downloading into me an immense wealth of knowledge, insight, assistance, guidance, and help at every single step of the publishing journey. May your patience and kindness be profoundly rewarded. Thank you will never seem enough to express my gratitude.

TABLE OF CONTENTS

Introduction	11
Identity	15
Completely	35
A Right Now Kind of God	43
That's What Daddies Do	55
The Breeding Ground of Fear	77
Morning Cups of Joy	105
Our Ugly Doesn't Scare God	119
Forgive and Forget, But…	145
Choices	171
Pigs in the Kitchen	185
Healthy Boundaries	203
All the Little Debbie Cakes	231
A Clean Slate	281
The Power of Connectivity	303
The Me That No One Sees	321
Imprinting	337
My Story, His Story	353

INTRODUCTION

COMPLETELY. Afterall, What Does It Even Mean? It is an attitude, a stance one takes - a lens through which one views life. It is our outlook, a place where we pitch our tent, and a platform. It is a place of support, a place of freedom, and a place of hope that cannot be snatched away by life's temporal circumstances. It is a place of choice, a place of deep joy, and a place that epitomizes and illustrates the heart of the Father. It is a place that is entirely accessible to all who dare journey into the unknown depths of its abyss. It is a place where we are called up higher from surviving to withstanding, from perishing to persevering, and from half-heartedness to resoluteness. It is a place marked by the indescribable trademark of God – a life that testifies to the evidence of God's fingerprints pointing to his unmistakable presence. It is a place where God blots out the existence of enemies from under heaven – for He alone is greater, grander, and the ultimate conqueror. It is a place where I declare, *If God is for me – then who dare even have the audacity to stand against me?!*

Is this your trademark? Are God's love and faithfulness a banner over your life?

Is God COMPLETELY in control of your all? As I drew closer to the completion and launch of this book, our Senior Pastor announced that his focus of the year was – COMPLETE SURRENDER. What a confirmation to my heart and soul about where God longs for His children to live.

What comes to mind when you ask yourself this question - **WHO AM I?** This question poses an exceptional and uncommon opportunity to dig deep and allow God to do some remarkable healing within us. I did not always see myself the way I do now, and if I were to be honest, sometimes I am still very much a work in progress in this area. If we are to live in complete freedom, we must offer up ourselves in complete surrender. We must ask ourselves the hard questions and pray the dangerous and difficult prayers that allow us to be vulnerable before an all-knowing, loving Father. Often, we proclaim we want to be free from the pain of our past while at the same time finding comfort within the familiar, confining, and restrictive walls of that pain. We find it too uncomfortable to sit with our discomfort, so we take every diversion that will distract us from the elephant in the room. Trusting the nature of God when we cannot see the hand of God takes radical faith and courage. Trusting that His parameters and guardrails are protective and not restrictive requires an essential and fundamental trust. Choosing to live a proactive life instead of a reactive life will be a drastic step towards purpose and destiny you will never regret - I promise. Stepping into the unknown gulfs of healing can be scary. But, if you dare to be courageous, believing that life can and will be different, then I can undoubtedly assure you this journey will be worth every tear shed and every mountain climbed. My hopes are as you read this memoir of my life and how God used each moment to develop and stretch me, that you will also see that God never abandoned me. Likewise, my friend, He has not abandoned you either. You are not alone in this thing we call life. We are stronger together! Let us begin.

CHAPTER 1
IDENTITY

There is value to be found in knowing our worth and value. If we do not understand our distinctiveness in Christ Jesus, lies and labels will seek to define who we are. If we do not know the truth, we will ultimately believe the lie.

When we become a Christ-follower, we take on the nature and identity of Christ. Our identity in Christ is part of our faith. The validity and great emphasis placed on the question posed in the introduction, **WHO AM I,** is supported in Scripture and reinforced by the very character we see in Christ. Recognizing and claiming our inherent identity in Christ is crucial in walking in and sustaining the freedom that God so desperately desires for us; the freedom Christ died for.

Christ has set us free to live a free life. So, take your stand! Never again let anyone put a harness of slavery on you. Galatians 5:1 MSG (The Message Translation)

If we never realize that we are children of the King, we will be doomed to walk through life as homeless vagabond amnesiacs never accessing our inheritance – and this mindset is right where the enemy of our souls would have us linger and camp out. Whether we choose to believe it or not has no bearing on the truth of its power, eminence, and application. There is a Heaven. There is a Hell. There is one true God. AND, there is an enemy of our soul fighting to take up precious real estate. Keeping us in bondage to our past fears, addictions, pain, disappointments, failures, deprived mindsets, generational bondages, and curses are only the tip of the iceberg when it comes to his tactics. He is ruthless and will stop at nothing. He has an arsenal filled with weapons; therefore, we would be wise to familiarize ourselves with the weapons of our warfare. Thankfully, our weapons are not of this world! They are supernatural. We are to use our God-weapons for assaulting and taking out the enemy. Battles fought in the natural with human weapons are exhausting and exasperating. Believe me, I know this firsthand. Battles fought on spiritual ground with power from above lift us beyond the storm to soar on the wings of eagles; protected and safeguarded from the windstorm beneath.

How blessed is God! And what a blessing he is! He's the Father of our Master, Jesus Christ, and takes us to the high places of blessing in him. Long before he laid down earth's foundations, he had us in mind, had settled on us as the focus of his love, to be made whole and holy by his love. Long, long ago he decided to adopt us into his family through Jesus Christ. (What pleasure he took in planning this!) He wanted us to enter into the celebration of his lavish gift-giving by the hand of his beloved Son. Ephesians 1: 3-6 MSG (The Message Translation)

This is more than just a beautiful and poetic sentiment. Think about it. Before time began. Before the foundations of the earth were even a thought, much less put into place to support life and creation. Before the first breath was breathed. Before any of it, He thought of me and you and made preparations for us. Before we ever were, He was, and we were on His mind and in His heart.

I was not always the woman you see before you today. Most would not have recognized me before my healing journey. There was a time when I saw myself as a small-town broken girl who had made far too many bad decisions and mistakes to ever see the light of day again.

The pit was deep.
The pit was dark.
The pit seemed hopeless.

Even worse, I saw myself as someone who did not deserve anything good to happen in her life; the girl who would spend the rest of her days in penance for all her wrongs. The girl who kept reverting to old patterns, old habits, and worn-out well-traveled roads. I had a pastor tell me one time, *"You have to get it right this time because YOU can't afford to make any more mistakes."* That statement haunted me for nearly 20 years and remains as vivid in my heart today as the day it was spoken over me;

HOWEVER, its power to control me has been washed by the Blood of Jesus. God's grace and power are always enough, period. End of story! There is nothing I can ever do to separate me from the love of my Father. It's not within my ability to comply and measure up, but rather in His enormous love for mankind. His mercies and love are brand new every single day.

I thought long and hard about this question, **WHO AM I,** because I had lived my entire life until this point in the shadows of this faulty belief system that hovered over me like a cloud every moment of every day. I saw myself as the mirror image of all the labels I wore; the sum total of all my past decisions and choices instead of the totality of God's amazing love and grace. These were labels I had placed on myself, labels others had placed upon me, and labels that had been passed down from one generation to the next.

Valerie, the girl who was emotionally, physically, and sexually abused.

Valerie, the girl always rejected and picked last; the one that no one wanted on their team. *(Especially in dodgeball. I think we all have some sort of elementary school dodgeball wounds we are carrying around if we were to be honest.)*

Valerie, the girl whose brother would not rescue her, often joining in with the bullies on the bus who daily tortured her both mentally and physically. *(To this day I still live with the long-term impact of a stack of hardcover textbooks being slammed down on top of my head from behind as hard as they could be. The pain was excruciating, and the sound shrilled through the air, yet no one gave notice, not even the bus driver. I never turned around to see my perpetrator. I did not need to because I knew who it was. I could hear their laughter. I simply fought the tears until I got off the bus.)*

Valerie, the girl who was unable to progress at the same pace as other students in baton class, and so was demoted to a younger class.

Valerie, the girl who completely lost her sense of all things musical in the middle of a piano recital performance, causing all those present to cringe in embarrassment for the poor little girl struggling at the piano. *(I somehow managed to regain my temporary lapse of memory before finishing the most unique and creative interpretation of Swanee River ever.)*

Valerie, the girl who always longed to be accepted and included but was always left off the party invite list.

Valerie, the girl whose second-grade teacher took a strong disliking of her and made it clear daily, always looking for ways to use her as an example to others. Valerie, the girl that would change schools one and a half years later only to find she would have to endure another school year with the very same teacher.

Valerie, a high school teen whose teachers pre-determined her academic performance and worth based on the previous performance of her older brother.

Valerie, the divorced single mom trying to make ends meet and always falling short.

Valerie, the single mom trying to raise a mentally ill and extremely violent child, in addition to another child with a severe physical and neurological medical diagnosis.

Valerie, the girl who struggled with alcohol addiction as a coping mechanism for life.

Valerie, the girl who always sought the approval and acceptance of others and would do whatever was required to receive it.

Valerie the girl who struggled with disordered eating, dis-regulated eating, food disorders, and food addictions.

Valerie, the mother of an incarcerated child.

Valerie, the chubby girl with the broom-straw unruly, thick, and frizzy hair.

Valerie, the girl with the terrible overbite and broken and missing teeth.

Valerie, the girl who did not have the latest fashions, name brands, or the trendiest clothes and jewelry that the other girls had.

Valerie, the young single mom whose naivety was taken advantage of and was tricked into a situation, being sexually approached, and touched by an Elder within the church.

Valerie, the piece of disposable trash that broken relationship after broken relationship had made her; whom society had branded her.

Valerie, the girl who would have to settle for whoever would have her now. *(The words of my grandfather held a power that day they were spoken that I would not realize until I was 40 years old.)*

Valerie, the girl with a big forehead.

Valerie, the girl who was becoming as big as the side of a house.

Valerie, the girl who was always overcome by embarrassment because of the harrowing truth that she could never do the pullups and pushups during P.E. class each year that others seemed to effortlessly excel at.

Valerie, the girl who became too tired to care anymore. The girl who could not wait to get away from the place she called home because at least somewhere else, anywhere else, they would not know the real Valerie.

Valerie, the girl who always longed for someone to step up and fight for her, yet no one ever did.

Valerie, the woman who tried to take her own life twice because the pain was far too great and the hurt ran too deep.

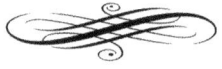

When I was expecting my second child, my daughter played softball on a local little league team. She was the one in the outfield sitting and playing with wildflowers and dirt instead of keeping her eye on the ball. One game she took her batting stance and I noticed the weeds sticking out of her back pocket. I could not help but giggle. She was not a natural-born athlete, but she loved being with her friends and that was all that mattered.

One evening the parents were standing around talking after practice, not paying too much attention to the group of six-year-old girls playing in the parallel field. The coach had already packed up all the equipment. In all our distraction, we had not noticed the girls had taken the balls back out of the bag and were playing again - that is until one came out of nowhere and smacked me right in the middle of my forehead.

Let me tell you - softballs are not soft and six-year-old girls can give any professional ball player a run for their money in ball speed. That hit took the breath completely out of me, knocking my five-month pregnant self off my feet and onto the ground. Thankfully another parent was right beside me and caught me, softening my ever-so-graceful descent. I was dazed, in shock, and confused. For a moment I could not hear anything and it seemed as if the entire ballfield was spinning. All the pain came rushing in at once.

Life is like this sometimes, you know? Unexpected disruptions fly out of nowhere and literally knock us off our feet and take our breath away. We are not even sure what has hit us. Perhaps we are even in a season of spiritual expectancy awaiting God's delivery of promise and purpose in our lives when the hit comes. Satan uses covert stealth tactics to catch us off guard to keep us from ever realizing our true identity and purpose. If he can attack our divine uniqueness, the very thing that sets us apart, through blind-siding us with curveball ambushes we never saw coming, then he can keep us in a position of fear, stunned paralysis, and spiritual concussions. It's impossible to catch the unexpected and disrupting curveballs of life we never see coming our way. We cannot fight unknown battles against invisible enemies. This is why it is critical to our survival and our ability to thrive to identify the enemy, recognize his tactics, plan accordingly, and have our guard up! Be proactive – not reactive. Have a game plan!

Identity is much like a state of being. When I was in elementary school, I used to tell people I had been adopted and that my name was Lucy. To this day I do not understand why I thought that was a great idea. I am certain there are many behaviors in life we do not have reasonable answers for, especially when talking about small children. One day I was called out on the lie by my mother. I remember her asking me why I would tell people such a thing. Honestly, I cannot remember my response or reasoning. However, this would not be the only time I would experience identity issues in life.

The thrill to the end of every school year was the arrival of the beloved school yearbook. We would flip through its pages trying to find how many times our picture would be displayed. We could not wait for all our friends to sign with the idyllic and iconic message of, **"Stay Cool, You Rule."** One year I was known as Valerie Harper all through the yearbook. The yearbook staff had failed to catch the mistake in the editing process. Simply known as *"Jake's little sister,"* yearbook staff wrongly assumed and listed me as Valerie Harper, the last name of another Jake in our school. Nowhere in the yearbook that year would I be listed under my true identity. Talk about feeling invisible and unseen. It might seem funny, and it was in some ways, but to be known as something or someone you are not is quite a big deal.

According to www.yourdictionary.com, we find that "identity" refers to who a person is – who they believe they are and how they think about themselves. Identity is a knowing, a recognition of aligning with something or someone. It is a sense of self and is the standard by which we judge and measure. Our identity gives us a sense of continuity, equipping us with stability to remain and persevere despite our circumstances or background. Identity establishes whole belief systems, developing and nurturing a person's confidence, character, self-worth, and sense of value. Whatever my identity is rooted in becomes the foundation upon which my entire life is built. I suppose you could say that identity is the infrastructure that gives the framework of life a sound, smooth, and unshakable footing.

The labels I wore were the framework of my life. They became the lens through which I viewed absolutely everything and the processor for all decisions and choices. This is why for much of my life I was easily led astray and often made extremely poor choices as a result. An inability to recognize truth and call out the lies will lead us down paths God never intended for us to travel. The labels I wore became the scaffolding of my life. I was an extremely fragile and volatile individual. I was all over the place, an emotional volcano waiting to erupt. My life was unpredictable and the hallmark of inconsistency, secrecy, and turbulence - despite my best efforts to put on the mask by which I became deceptively recognized.

Taking charge of the dialogue between my ears and refusing to allow the enemy to take up precious real estate in my life took a lot of courage and determination. It took a lot of hard work that seemed like it would never end. It was not a quick fix. My mind was a combat zone. Writing about this journey is a piece of my heart, broken and spilled out for all to see in hopes that it will encourage others to believe they are of immense value and worth to their Creator. He desperately wants us to take hold of our true identity in Him. We were all created on purpose and by design to **Know God, Find Freedom, Discover Purpose, and Make a Difference.** This is my story of that very truth and revelation that our Senior Pastor, Chris Hodges at Church of the Highlands, has made the heartbeat of our church. Never has this profound truth been more revealing of the nature and heart of God than right now. So, what labels have I used to replace the ones we previously read about? I am so glad you asked.

I am a wonderful wife.

I am a great mother.

I am a loving grandmother.

I am a blessed daughter.

I am an understanding and tender sister.

I am an adoring aunt.

I am a fun, family-loving, God-fearing, chicken-wing-loving, people-loving, march-to-the-beat-of-my-very-own-drum kind of girl.

I am a DIY enthusiast, a home gardener want-to-be, and a traveling and hiking junkie fanatic.

I'm an eye-ball-it kind of free spirit who loves creating.

I am a coffee-loving, faithful sappy Hallmark Christmas-movie-watching, monogram-loving kind of soul.

I am a Class II rapids, play it sort of safe with a little adventure mixed in kind of rebel heart.

I am a re-purposer *(Is that even a word?)* of all things broken, believing that dead bones can live again and joy can rise from the ash piles of life.

I am a documentary-loving, statistics-looking-upper kind of gal.

I am a beautiful, loved, treasured, and adored daughter of the King of ALL Kings.

I am intelligent and I have much to bring to the table.

I am chosen, redeemed, strong, courageous, and desired.

I am beloved and cherished, not a disposable and throw-a-way girl.

I am a warrior child of a warrior King.

I am an overcomer bought and paid for by the ransom of Blood spilled on the Cross.

I am heard, I am anointed, I am capable, I am equipped, I am called, and I am valued.

I am not invisible but seen by God himself.

I am accepted by the One who matters the most.

I do not always agree with the mainstream, I often laugh when I should not, and I love living in my own little bubble of isolation and perfection. More on that later. *(God has done some amazing revelations and healing in my life in this area.)*

My husband calls me Babe.

My children call me Mom.

My stepchildren and other family members call me Valerie.

My grandbabies call me ViVi, except for our Ellie-girl, and she will forever call me MiMi.

My friends call me VJ or Val.

I have learned in life that humanity will fail me, I will fail me, things will fail me, and government will fail me. My church will fail me, culture will fail me, standards will fail me, and people and systems will fail me. But - God will never fail me. God is very well acquainted with my humanity. After all, I am created in His likeness and His image. He loves me on my best days, and He loves me on my worst days when I cannot stand myself. In the moments when words seem to fail me, He hears the prayers my lips cannot seem to formulate words to pray. He is faithful like that!

This story is a journey of reflections, revelations, redemptions, and Red Sea and Damascus Roads along the way. It is about learning what it truly means to abide, in every sense of the way – Completely! It is about learning to till dirt while waiting to plant seeds. It's about coming to the resolve that sometimes we do not get to see the harvest. But mostly, it is about falling in love with my Father; every single day, over and over and over.

It is about His great love, His far-reaching mercy, His devoted tenderness, and His beautiful nature. It is about learning that my story is mostly about HIM, not me.

CHAPTER 2
COMPLETELY

Merriam-Webster online dictionary defines the word COMPLETELY as having all of the necessary parts, elements, or steps. It's an absolute, a thoroughness, a conclusive and highly proficient condition. Merriam-Webster goes on to further define COMPLETELY as a perfected state, to mark the end of something, to execute, to fulfill, or to carry out a task successfully.

COMPLETELY is about a journey to real unadulterated truth, God's truth. It is the crossing over from mere wandering and wondering to finding assurance within the pages of promises found in God's love letters to His daughter. It is a discovery of a beautiful and redemptive love story tucked between the pages and dotted through many Red Sea Road moments. It's a journey that leads to fulfillment rooted in hope both sustainable and life-giving. It is a story about the miraculous delivery of a child in seemingly impossible and impassible moments of life. It is about discovering identity and exposing all of the defective, distorted, and flawed foundational systems a life had been built upon. It is about taking all of the inoperative components of a life and allowing God to validate them; taking brokenness and breathing new life into it.

COMPLETELY marks an end to self-reliance. A genesis begins with pure and absolute raw honesty, persistent determination, and a strength that can only be found in perseverance – in a total reliance upon God. Learning to abide COMPLETELY will require that you discover your wings and learn to fly, instead of looking for the nearest branch to rest upon. Your story will not look exactly like mine, although I can imagine there are many resemblances and similarities. I believe we are more alike than we know. The hope of my heart is that you will find encouragement and perhaps even inspiration as you dive into these pages. My hopes are you will not feel so alone in your journey after reading this portrait of God's faithfulness. You might even find yourself proclaiming – *YOU MEAN, I'M NOT THE ONLY ONE?* Perhaps, just maybe, you will discover the value to be found and held dear in knowing your personal value and worth.

    I am certain I am not qualified to write a book of this nature, or perhaps any book at all for that matter. I do not have a college education, and I am sure my editors have cringed at my use of punctuation along with my lengthy sentences and sentence structures. On the other hand, who is more qualified than me? The funny thing about the nature of our God is that He loves to qualify the unqualified. He is not looking for perfection. Just like He chose to reveal the birth of Christ to a bunch of overlooked and unaccepted shepherds by the standards of their day, His grace too will take us where only His presence can sustain us. We must learn to trust His nature even when we cannot understand or see what He is doing in our lives in the natural. His power in our lives positions us perfectly for such a time as this.

I'm a simple girl from a small Alabama town. As a child, I was filled with social anxiety and would look like a bull raring to charge anyone who had the audacity to even think about glancing my way. Life's demands and professional responsibilities would find a way to pull me out of my shell, but putting myself "out there" has never come easy. I don't think it will ever be "easy" for me – my thorn in the side I suppose. It is a daily choice to be present and not to isolate. Many of my close friends do not see me in this capacity, but they never met the girl who would nearly pull her mother's skirt off trying to hide under it either.

> **God has seen fit
> to place a deep desire within me
> *to pull out of me*
> all that He has deposited within me.**

If my life can reflect His goodness, His nature, and His Glory, and bring Heaven to Earth for even just one - then this place of vulnerability is worth every sacrifice, every tear, every prayer, and most of all - every moment of the journey. May I never waste this journey. May I never waste the moments. May I never waste the seasons of waiting. Let me encourage you as you dive in - begin with a time of worship, a time of reflection, and a time of asking God to reveal things hidden to you. Pray that He will lead you in the ways of the everlasting as you read and draw close to Him. Wisdom and revelation are given to those who ask. I pray you will have the courage to pray the hard prayers and trust in God's loving and gracious nature to bring you to a place of freedom.

> *Father God, in the name of Jesus, and by the power of the Holy Spirit, we submit this time together to You. We ask that You do that which only You can do. We consecrate these moments spent reading to You and ask that You mend all that is broken within us, heal what is damaged within us, and restore what is lost to us. Ignite understanding within us through the power of truth, connection, testimony, and through the Blood of Jesus. May we surrender our will to Your will and trust You with our hopes and dreams. May You give us the courage to have open hearts, open hands, and open minds. Ignite vision and purpose within us. Awaken us. Revive us. Repair us. Restore us. Renew us. Redeem us. Heal us. Massage our hearts back to life Father. Help us to choose abundant life and freedom. Quinch that which thirst within us. Help us to release and fully trust in You and Your plan. Satisfy our longings. Satiate the hunger within*

us. Fill us with Your peace that is beyond human comprehension. Break old habits and patterns, and replace them with a new way – YOUR WAY. Give us wisdom and insight. Enable us to fulfill the purpose You have created us for. Walk with us and guide us by Your Holy Spirit. Show us Your ways continually and be a light unto the path You are leading us down.

Reveal the truth to us. Enlighten Holy Scripture to us. Expose the enemy and his lies for what they are. Give us a spirit of understanding and remove the scales of deception from our eyes. Empower us. Give us confidence. Remind us continually of our heritage. Lead us in the way of the everlasting and allow us to see the goodness of You, our loving and most devoted Father, in the land of the living. Father, we know as we courageously begin this journey to complete surrender that chains are going to be broken off our lives. We believe that the layers of hurt upon hurt will begin to be peeled back. We trust that as walls begin to fall, You are setting us free to possess our promised land. We thank You, Father, knowing You are a good Father. We thank you because we know that You are for us! In Jesus name, Amen!

CHAPTER 3
A RIGHT NOW KIND OF GOD

As I have grown older, I have come to the realization that my teenage and young-adult self held my parents to unattainable standards with my unrealistic and self-promoting expectations. My parents always did the best they could with the upbringing and training they had, although in my formative years, I may not have understood nor appreciated this nugget of truth. They never wanted us to experience the kind of upbringing they had to endure. They worked selflessly to give us a better life than they had. I am extremely grateful for the upbringing I had. Knowing one is loved beyond measure is the best gift a child could ever hope for. This is the gift my parents gave me.

I have one older brother and we grew up in iconic small-town Americana. My hometown looks like it was ripped straight from the pages of a Hallmark script. The town of Columbiana was home to approximately 3,400 residents when I graduated from Shelby County High School. The main road through town is home to odds-and-ends variety shops, antique stores, a coffee house, a barber shop, and the iconic Davis Drug Store, complete with the soda fountain. At the end of this street is the old original Shelby County Courthouse, built in 1854 and now standing as a museum filled with yesteryear's memorabilia and days-gone-by town history. Columbiana is the county seat, and the new

Court House sits further down on the same main street that runs through the center of town. It is a beautiful little town where everybody knows everyone, literally.

Growing up, Fridays were filled with the excitement of getting out of classes early for pep rallies, football game preparations, homecoming parades, and dances following home games. As with most southern small towns, high school football season was the height of excitement. I was in the band for five years, where I played the flute for two years, participated in the Color-guard for three years, serving as Captain of the Color-guard/Dance-line Squad my junior year. This was the first year we were successful in convincing our Band Director to allow dancing outside of the majorette line. We were thrilled as we performed our hearts out to *"Great Balls of Fire."* My senior year of high school I decided to drop out of band to work, saving to buy my first car. My first car was an orangey-red, two-door, 1986 Mustang LX. I loved that little car and thought I was hot stuff. My payments were around $117 per month and gas was around $1.11 per gallon. Life was sweet and I had newfound freedom. This girl was on the move. Our weekend activities included driving in circles, very slowly, through the parking lot of the local Taco Bell and Hardees - all while staring at one another, yet trying to not get caught actually staring at one another. You have not lived until you've experienced this adventurous night on the town. I have many memories of this small town. Some memories I wish I could hold onto forever, memories for which I am incredibly grateful. I also have other memories I wish I could develop a permanent case of amnesia for. I'm sure we all do.

I have come to realize that all those memories and experiences helped shape and form me into the woman that I have become. God has used every heartache and lesson along the way to develop a core filled with an unshakeable, always expanding, and unbreakable strength. He has used these experiences as a catapult to thrust me into a life of purpose, hope, and destiny. It is a life filled with beautiful opportunities I never could see before now. It is only at this point in my life that I understand the value to be found in knowing my personal value and understanding my purpose.

I pray that He may grant you, according to the riches of His glory, to be strengthened with power in the inner man through His Spirit, and that the Messiah may dwell in your hearts through faith. I pray that you, being rooted and firmly established in love, may be able to comprehend with all the saints what is the length and width, height and depth of God's love, and to know the Messiah's love that surpasses knowledge, so you may be filled with all the fullness of God. Now to Him who is able to do above and beyond all that we ask or think according to the power that

works in us— to Him be glory in the church and in Christ Jesus to all generations, forever and ever. Amen.
Ephesians 3:16-21 Holman Christian Standard Bible (HCSB)

I love this passage of Scriptures. As I sit here and ponder the tenderness of Paul's prayer, I cannot help but think over my own life. One day when I was reading, I had a moment that forever changed how I will read this passage of Scriptures. It came alive to me. I used to read it with the emphasis as **"Now to HIM,"** but now I read it with a dual emphasis, **"<u>NOW</u> to <u>HIM</u>!"**

It is **NOW**.
It is **Today**.
Not Yesterday.
Not Tomorrow.
Right **NOW**.

Right **NOW,** in this moment. Right here and right **NOW His** presence is drawing attention to my life as **He** rewrites the narrative, as **He** orders my steps, and guides me by **His** Holy Spirit. Because of **His NOW**ness, **He** deserves all the praise, all the glory, all the acclamations, and all my admiration. Right **NOW,** I give **HIM** ALONE all the honor, all the glory, and all my respect. Right **NOW,** in my every day, walking around life.

In my mom life.
In my wife and married life.
In my grandmother life.
In my professional life.
In my church life.
In my broken life.
In my home life.
In my health journey life.
In my non-profit work life.
In my writing life.
In my prayer life.
In my sister life.
In my daughter life.

NOW! He is a **NOW** God! Not a has been or used to be God. In all these moments and seasons that make up this thing we call life, God is ABLE right **NOW**! My **NOW** God deserves all my praise and all tribute goes to **Him**. He goes beyond what my mind can fathom. He goes beyond what my intellect can handle. Because of this undeniable truth, God has woven together all the pieces of my life into a beautiful tapestry. **NOW** – I was created for such a time as this, by design, intentionally, with immense value and purpose. No one can do what I was put on this earth to do except for me.

Let us look at the first part of that passage again.

I pray that He may grant you, according to the riches of His glory, to be strengthened with power in the inner man through His Spirit, and that the Messiah may dwell in your hearts through faith. I pray that you, being rooted and firmly established in love, ... Ephesians 3:16-17, Holman Christian Standard Bible (HCSB)

When something is strengthened, it is in essence reinforced, intensified, increased, or braced. It is empowered. What an incredible thought that God desires we be reinforced by power and strength – braced and propped up by power within the complexities of our innermost being. A quick Google search through online dictionaries will render numerous results for the words "inner man." The "inner man" we often refer to as our soul can also represent our core, our ego, or our heart. God desires that we be wired and reinforced with power and strength in the very core of who we are, that our self-esteem be deeply rooted in the knowledge that we belong to the **NOW** God of the Angel Armies. God longs for our self-worth, our confidence, as well as our psyche to be wrapped around the very idea that no other power outside of God could ever stand in comparison. Why? Because no weapon formed against God's children will flourish and succeed. When we get a choke-hold on the reality of this **NOW** power, when we grab onto it and refuse to let go - then we can understand the extreme vastness of His infinite love that surrounds us right **NOW**.

It does not take much for me to get distracted if I'm not careful. Without intentional effort placed on focusing, I will find my way down a rabbit hole faster than minnows swimming around in the minnow vat at the bait shop my Little Mama and Daddy Cups used to own. Satan will use any means possible to keep us distracted. For me, distractions came in the form of heartbreak, loss, relationships, busyness, food addiction and disorders, substance abuse, temple demolition, suicidal ideation and attempts, and abuse.

My life has been dotted with seasons of not providing my body, mind, and spirit with what was needed to sustain overall optimal health. Due to my unsound lifestyle, lack of physical activity, and poor diet choices, as well as a genetic predisposition, I found myself in a very dark place. The extreme muscle weakness and atrophy, severe fatigue, and widespread emotional, mental, and spiritual exhaustion left me in a state of acute debilitation. Life was happening to me and all around me, instead of me making my mark on life. Have you ever seen those tube man inflatables businesses use as attention grabbers? That was me! I was all over the place. In fact, I was so exhausted and weak that a small gust of wind could have blown me completely over. My emotional and mental stability was being fueled by a diet rich in toxic and chemical-laden foods, fast foods, refined flours, and highly processed and addictive sugars. I was living off eight (sometimes more) Diet Dr. Peppers a day. I used to call Diet Dr. Pepper the nectar of Heaven, God's gift to me. To put it simply, I was a mess. My spiritual connection to God and others was non-existent. We were designed to live life within a protective layer of something called community. We were never designed to go through life alone. The problem was this though - I did not care for people in general. This is raw honesty folks - and this mindset was a problem!

God has used these moments and seasons in my life to fulfill His promise of a hopeful future He planned for me long before the foundations of the earth were ever laid. He planned to be a **NOW** God for all the **NOW** moments of my life before time began y'all. Think about that. He was showing up for us before we were ever born.

For we are God's masterpiece. He has created us anew in Christ Jesus, so we can do the good things he planned for us long ago. Ephesians 2:10 NLT

As God looked down throughout all eternity and saw all the moments of my life, good and bad, He still loved me and He has always desired His best for me. He loved me so much that He pre-decided to send His only son, Jesus Christ, on a rescue mission before I had ever taken my first breath. He has used all the moments of my life to display His **NOW** Glory and **His** truest nature to my heart – the nature of a good Father who only wants what is best for me.

For I know the plans I have for you, says the LORD. They are plans for good and not for disaster, to give you a future and a hope. Jeremiah 29:11 NLT

And we know that God causes everything to work together for the good of those who love God and are called according to his purpose for them. Romans 8:28 NLT

*Father, In the name of your son Jesus, and by the power of the Holy Spirit, please peel back the layers - one at a time – and allow us to see You right here and right **NOW**. Help us to believe that You are good and that You desire the best for us. Help us to grasp hold of the truth that nothing can ever separate us from Your love. May we allow Your nature and identity to take root in our hearts and go deep into all the dark recesses bringing healing and revealing virtue. May we never forget that You are a right **NOW** God who is working in ways perhaps we cannot always see, but that we can always trust. May we always trust Your nature, knowing we are on Your heart; knowing we were the heart of the cross. In Jesus Name, Amen.*

CHAPTER 4
THAT'S WHAT DADDIES DO

My Dad passed away in March of 2022, just two and a half weeks before what would have been his 74th birthday. I cannot help but imagine all the moments we will miss him being a part of; all the milestones in the lives of his grandchildren and great-grandchildren. It's hard to accept I'll never be making banana pudding for him again, or taking him a gift at Christmas, Father's Day or his Birthday. Even more inconceivable are the thoughts of all the ordinary, everyday moments without him that seem to creep by. A while back I was shopping in a thrift store, one of my favorite pastimes, when I saw a pair of men's overalls hanging on the rack. Daddy was a short man and these looked like the perfect length and size for his short and stocky stature. I reached out to grab them, then I caught myself and gently pulled my hand back. Daddy was a huge fan of my cornbread dressing during the Holidays. It simply would not do if I forgot to bring along the canned, jellied cranberry sauce he loved as well. He wanted a whole can just for himself. He loved his barn on the hill, the "man cave" he called it. He had waited his entire life to have his barn, working endless hours, and now he reaped the rewards of his hard work.

    I have often wondered why we could not have had more years with Daddy. Learning to navigate earth without his presence has been difficult to temper with the reality that this is simply an obstacle

I cannot maneuver around. It is an experience I must process and move through. I knew in my spirit that the fall of 2021 would be our last Holiday season with him. There have been times in my life where I could clearly sense God's gentle preparation of my heart for an upcoming climb. This was one of those moments.

Mom and Dad were married for nearly 50 ½ years. Sometimes I feel like we lost Mom the same day that Dad passed. Grieving the physical loss of my Dad while at the same time grieving the emotional loss of my Mom has been a challenging season – for both her and me. While I am intimately acquainted with the grief associated with the loss of my Dad, I have no frame of reference for what it must be like to lose your spouse of half a century. I have been required to be a pillar of strength when I have felt more like a mound of sand. Grief is a precarious thing. It is shaky, unstable, uncertain, and an uninvited part of life by most. It fills its victims with insecurity and is unreliable at best. The unpredictable and unreasonable nature of grief can make the mere task of breathing seem unattainable at times. If not for the grace of God, I don't think I could have walked this road of loss. Yet, here I am today. This piece of evidence points to the undeniable rhythms of grace that hold me steady during unsettling and unwanted storms of life.

Daddy never held me to impossible standards. He simply loved the best he knew how. He was a simple man, a down-home country boy and kid at heart. He had a harsh life growing up. These are stories he didn't openly share with many. Although he knew he was loved, he often felt he was in the way. He was never allowed to have an opinion that differed from that of the adults in his life. Because of this, Dad never learned how to form opinions of his own until he was well into adulthood. Daddy's home life lacked gentle grace and was often militant. There was always work to be done, which left very little time to simply be a child. Children were to do what they were told, when they were told, exactly how they were told - without any exceptions or unsolicited opinions. As they grew into young teenagers, the Harris boys had built themselves quite a reputation for being wild. Through the years Daddy managed to break free from the impact of his upbringing, slowly developing a more soothing approach to life as he grew older. He became softer-spoken, a man of his word, and a man of impeccable character. His reputation preceded him as a man who could be trusted. All who knew him respected him. He truly left me a legacy of love.

I watched those last few weeks as my Daddy slowly slipped into the hands of Jesus, passing from this life into the eternal. It was one of the most beautiful things while also being one of the hardest and most heartbreaking moments I have ever had to experience. I simply could not imagine a world where my Daddy did not exist, nor did I want to. Watching this man who was the epitome of strength be rendered completely helpless seemed like a cruel joke on humanity to my natural mind. One night as he lay in his hospital bed shaking from toxins his liver could not filter, I watched as he lifted his bruised and weak arms toward Heaven. He spoke the name of Jesus over and over with every ounce of strength he had remaining. He said, *"Jesus, I see you."* We brought him home from the hospital five days before he passed. All he wanted was to sit in his chair, covered with his favorite red buffalo-checked fleece blanket we had given him for Christmas a few years earlier, and to drink ice-cold water from his favorite stainless-steel mug. His body was so weakened by disease and toxicity that he could not do even the most basic things for himself.

As I look back on these last days with my Dad, I realize that I had not fully come to terms with the fact it was his time to go meet Jesus. I had not allowed my heart to fully believe what my mind already knew, that we were about to see him on earth for the final time. Perhaps it was self-preservation so I could be strong for my Mom and make sure all the details were taken care of. Daddy slipped into a coma in those final days as we spent hours sitting by him, holding his extremely swollen hands. We watched as simply breathing took every ounce of strength he could muster up. Despite oxygen assistance, his chest rose and fell in harsh rhythmic patterns. We talked with him so he would know he was not alone. Hospice had already told us sometimes people, especially men, will hold on as long as they can out of a fear that their family will suffer. Because of this, we whispered into his ears that we loved him and it was okay to go with Jesus, assuring him we would be okay. Those words felt like the most inhumane, cold-blooded utterance I had ever made – despite their intentions to ease my Dad's pain and give him peace. I sang *Daddy's Hands* in his ears as tears rolled down my cheeks. *(This was a special song between me and my Dad. We played a recording of me singing it at his funeral.)* I will never forget walking into his bedroom on March 6th at 9:43 PM and finding he was no longer with us. His chest was not moving. He was not gasping for air. His body hard and cold. The only sound was that of the oxygen machine. That moment is forever stamped upon my heart. Waking my mom and daughter, and calling my brother and husband - all moments that still somehow seem like a dream in my mind.

I remember my Dad as a man of integrity who loved his family and friends, loved God, worked hard, and mostly kept to himself. He knew how to command attention with his very presence, but also had a natural bent to fade into the backdrop. This was his preference and I am certain where I get it from. He never loved being the center of anyone's attention, except my Mom's of course. He could cut up with the best of them, but you felt the sting of his disapproval when pushed too far. I recall Daddy prancing around the house in Mom's wig, her house dress, and even her bra one time. Yes, you read that correctly. He was a ham! Daddy loved to answer the landline telephone as "Shelby County Sherriff's Office," or "Joe's Morgue, You Stab'em, We Slab'em." As inappropriate as that was, I cannot help but remember his hysterical laugh when the caller on the other end would hang up, especially if they happened to be a boy I was interested in. That is, until one time the FOP was on the other end of the line asking for their annual donation. You better believe Daddy pledged a donation that year – a generous donation at that. Caller ID would have been useful in those days!

    Daddy loved to scare my boyfriends and was not afraid to send them packing when his little girl gave any indication that she was not interested. He was also notorious for poking fun at me and my brother when we would get into trouble. One time he got himself put in the corner along with us for cutting up a bit too much. Of course, my brother and

I thought that was the funniest ever! Daddy never drank once my brother and I came along. You would never be able to accuse him of gossip. His worst vice I can remember was his love for Winchester miniature cigars, which he always smoked outside. Daddy was far from perfect, but he was always one to give others the benefit of a doubt, believing a person was innocent until they proved otherwise. Even then, he was quick to forgive and move on. This grace nature of his was one we would experience time and time again. Daddy did not hold grudges, a nature that grew deeper and wider in him as he grew to understand the dimensions of the love of Jesus more and more. He would give you the shirt off his back, even if it was the last shirt he owned. If he did not own a shirt, he would find a way to get you a shirt without regard to his own need. This is a picture of the love of God made evident in a broken man's life.

Daddy was not a man of many words and usually cut straight to the chase, often not knowing how to express love or how to season his speech. I realize now it wasn't that he didn't love us; he just didn't know how to show it other than to work hard and provide. He was raised in a punitive environment with an extremely strict mother and a father who would not be up for any daddy-of-the-year awards. I do not know much about my Dad's maternal side of the family, other than his Mother had been raised in a harsh and critical environment as well. In her later years she began to soften around the edges, breaking free from some of the lifelong impacts her harsh upbringing had on her. My Dad's father and his siblings had been orphaned as small children and split up. Some were never seen again. I cannot imagine what that must have been like. My Little Mama (Dad's Mom) was diligent in taking care of her home. She loved her home and always had an open door, showing her love by preparing food for anyone who came through those open doors. I have many wonderful memories of sitting around the living room while she crocheted a blanket and watched her stories (soap operas), of her making cathead biscuits and cornbread, the eternal boiler of butter beans on the stove, and that undeniable trademarked homemade vanilla ice cream of hers. I never knew Daddy Louie (Dad's dad) very well. I met him a few times when I was very young and have heard stories, but never had an actual relationship with him.

For as long as I can remember Dad worked many long hours. He worked when he was sick. He worked on weekends. He worked on holidays. He worked when he was tired. He worked side jobs and odd jobs. I recall Momma loading us kids and dinner into the car one dark and cold Christmas Eve when he was working as a nightshift dispatcher for a trucking company. We spent that Christmas Eve in the dirty and greasy garage bay of Southern Haulers in Calera, Alabama, so we could be together. We waited until Daddy got home the next morning to have Christmas, and then he went to bed to sleep for a few hours.

This was normal for us. I grew up thinking that men worked all the time – ALL OF THE TIME - and women took care of absolutely everything else – the house, the kids, the finances, the discipline, the extracurricular activities, trips, planning, decisions for the family, etc. Daddies left before sunrise and came home after dark. Daddies broke the rules and mommas were the enforcers of rules. I can still hear my Dad saying, *"If you don't behave, your Momma is going to spank you."* This lens through which I viewed a father figure shaped the lens through which I also viewed my Heavenly Father. I saw God as the "big guy" in Heaven ruling over everything and taking care of us. He provided for all our needs. All we had to do was give Him our list. Our job was to take care of everything else down here. He was far too busy working to bother himself with the cares of everyday life. Simply honor God, be respectful, have fun, and do not get in the way. This is a pattern I saw play out in church as well.

For the first nearly twelve years of my life, we attended a small country Baptist church not far from our home. Our tiny church was surrounded by lush pasture fields and planted smack dab in the middle of nowhere, literally. I have many memories of this church, like the time I got locked inside after service and in a panic nearly broke down the church doors to escape the cold and dark dungeon. Talk about dramatic hysterics. I was only about five years old at the time and was certain this was doomsday and my life was over – so, I should be given a pass on the drama.

Church was traditional in that we had Sunday School, complete with flannel-graphs of all the Bible stories, followed by a traditional service where we sang congregational song selections from the beloved red-back hymnal. My parents have always loved the red-back hymnal. They have even been known to select a church home based on the hymnal book used. It held and still holds a treasure trove of memories for them, as well as for me. *"Love Lifted Me"* was one of my favorites and I wanted to sing it every Sunday when I was a little girl. Sometimes we would have Testimonial Sunday - the entire service dedicated to congregation members standing to testify of the goodness of God, and of how much they loved the Lord and His faithfulness. I usually ended up on the floor wallowing under the pews barefooted because I hated shoes, and if being honest, because I was bored. This is probably how I was overlooked and ended up locked in the dark church that one Sunday night.

Mrs. Ettress lived across the field a good distance from where we lived at the time. One Sunday night I recall her testimony of how she had heard me singing at the top of my lungs from across the field, *"He's Still Working on Me."* Although my sweet innocent voice being carried on the wings of the wind had ministered to her, I was feeling quite humiliated and uncomfortable with all eyes on me. I wanted to disappear between the fibers of the carpet. Unfortunately, I couldn't seem to squeeze myself into the spaces between those fibers – but that did not stop me from trying.

Once a year, Homecoming rolled around. Oh, how we loved Homecoming at church. It was almost as exciting as Old-Fashion Day. Envision Pollyanna and you will just about have the scene set perfectly in your mind. This was a special day. A day looked forward to all year long and planned for months in advance. You wore your best dress, including your knee-high white socks. No big brother hand-me-downs on this day! Homecoming Sunday meant copious amounts of food spread down the concrete slab tables underneath the pavilion. It seemed like that table was a mile long and filled with every tastebud-tickling fancy known to man. To my little mind, it seemed to be enough food to feed the entire world. The Keto police were not in attendance. The Carnivore Nation was not present. No one was counting macros, calories, fat, or sodium, nor was there anyone worried about bacteria growth, food spoilage, or food temperature. No one was quoting the CDC, HHS, USDA, or FDA guidelines. I'm not sure many of us even knew there was such organizations and regulations. All the food was set out on the tables upon arrival and stayed there most of the day. Funny thing is, I don't ever recall anyone getting sick. I mostly remember all the foods that we rarely got to enjoy at home on our $10 per week grocery budget at the time. My Mom could stretch a dollar till it hollered. She was a saint at providing food for her family. Our diet at home consisted of oatmeal for breakfast, peanut butter & jelly sandwiches for lunch, and those round butter cookies for a snack – you know, the ones you could stick on your fingers like rings. Dinner was mostly beans and cornbread, meat once or twice per week, potatoes, and any garden goodies mom had grown and preserved. We drank water, Kool-Aid on occasion, and milk from a dairy farm Daddy knew about. It was not until we got older and Mom started working outside the home consistently that our grocery budget would increase - and our waistlines along with it. I think this is why Homecoming lunch was my most looked-forward-to event of the year because it meant we got to enjoy foods we rarely ever had at home.

Homecoming also meant a good old-fashion singing following lunch. It was an all-day affair with no evening service planned. I always did love singings at church. I loved the harmonies and the variations in melodies and tones, and sat on the edge of the pew waiting to see how long they could hold out that last note before passing out or turning blue. As the last note was carried into oblivion, everyone would explode in accolades of praise.

Although children and young adults were valued, a focused and intentional effort geared towards spiritual training was never a matter of prominence in our small church. Children were adored, no doubt, but the unstated, silent rule of thumb stood - children were to be seen and not heard. I do recall a short period of time when my Mom and her best friend tried to organize and lead the teen/young adults at church. Of course, without much support overall it was doomed to be short-lived. It is sad to admit, but to this day there's not much of anything we were taught in Sunday School or services that have been substantial contributors to my spiritual maturity and growth. I do remember always being assigned as the angel who sang *"Silent Night"* in the Christmas program. To this day I don't fancy that song. It seems almost "wrong" to say I do not like a song about the birth of Christ, but here we are again with raw honesty.

We used to ask to go the bathroom during service so we could sneak out into the surrounding cow pasture fields and play, and then hurry back before we had been gone long enough that Mom noticed. Parents were not afraid to take kids outside the church and apply the board of education to the seat of understanding either. Sometimes you could see this play out through the windows of the church, depending on where you were sitting that particular Sunday. It was a walk of shame when you re-entered the church if you were the one on the receiving end of the spanking. Most memorable would be those children proclaiming loudly, *"no Momma, no,"* as they were escorted out of the church to receive their due punishment.

I recall singing my first solo in this small country church as well, accompanied by my mother on the keys – *He's Still Working on Me* – a song that is still engraved on my heart to this day. I can remember standing by her at the piano as I belted out the song, a song I didn't understand, but that Momma had been teaching me. She had bought an old antique Singer piano in a yard sale for $50 and taught herself to chord using it. Mom was always very resourceful and talented - and still has the voice of a songbird to this day.

I suppose one of my most vivid memories, however, is of a little girl named Lela who always had the prettiest and ruffliest dresses. Oh, how I wanted to have dresses like Lela. Everyone always doted over how pretty she looked. They were the kind of dresses that would swirl around you in a cloud of lace when you twirled. My dresses were always beautiful and mostly handsewn in love by my Momma, who always made sure I was dolled up for church. Growing up my Mom had always longed for pretty dresses, but they never seemed to have money for frivolous expenditures such as that. At my tender young age, I couldn't appreciate the value in my dresses and the comparison game took root. As pretty as my dresses were, they were not like Lela's dresses and no one ever poured over how pretty I looked in them. I longed for a dress with so many ruffles that it engulfed my entire body. I recall the only time anyone ever said much about my appearance was the time my MaMaw gave me a perm without my Mother's permission. She finally brought me home a week later and did the infamous doorbell ditch. I'm pretty sure she created the doorbell ditch. She left me on the front steps, quickly knocking on the door, then scurried back to her car, and in a flash was driving away when Mom opened the door. My MaMaw knew she had messed up. It's probably a good thing that cell phones and texting didn't exist back then. Mind you this perm had been in my hair for a week by this time, yet my Mother still tried to wash it out with green Palmolive dish soap, or at least that is how I remember it. It seemed like hours I was bent over that tub on the receiving end of her frustration, anger, and determination. I was teased and called "Little Orphan Annie" by grown adults at church. I'm sure they didn't mean any harm. I am positively certain they didn't mean any harm - but to my little mind it was another nail in the coffin of rejection and self-image dialogues and arguments I would start having internally about my worth and identity.

Although I did not realize it at the time, Satan was using these seemingly harmless moments to build lies upon lies and to strengthen the worst of what I already believed to be truths about my identity. As a young child, I learned to adapt to and nurse my hurt feelings of being excluded or overlooked. Mostly I felt invisible and unworthy of attention. I thought Lela was the bar I needed to reach for perfection, beauty, and acceptance. As I grew older, I soon found there would always be a Lela in my life. As an adult, I am absolutely certain that little Lela knew nothing of this and was in no way an accessory to this crime and my misery. But, at the time, I felt like I was in constant competition with her.

I suppose the biggest thing I remember was the men at church seemed to be just like my Daddy, except my Daddy was King in my book! The men of the church took care of business. They did the "big work" and the "important stuff," while the women were there to support and take care of the men. The women took care of all the little details they were too busy to be occupied with. Women were frowned upon if they spoke up and gave their opinion on anything, especially in a business meeting. This was unheard of, as my Mom would find out one ill-fated evening when she forgot to mention she was speaking on behalf of my Dad, per his request of course, since he was unable to attend due to work. It was also frowned upon if women wore pants anywhere on the premises of the church and its property. To do so was a sign of being worldly, although it was perfectly acceptable to wear pants outside of the premises of the church. This was a contradiction my little mind had a difficult time processing. Supposedly, it was believed that women refusing to dress "appropriately" alluded to an evil spirit of rebellion. This rebellious spirit threatened an insurgence of estrogen that would surely destroy the anointing and the pulpit. A woman wearing pants was viewed as disrespectful to God and communicated a refusal to submit to authority – but only while at the church or on church grounds of course. The wrath my Mom's best friend would unfortunately experience after showing up wearing slacks one evening would become the straw that broke the camel's back.

God would call my family to change church homes when I was almost twelve years old. This decision would be the start of my deconversion, my loss of faith (faith as I knew and understood it then anyways). Fractures to my developing spirit and heart penetrated deep by this point. How I viewed male roles, female roles, and God's role in my life had been systematically reinforced for nearly twelve years on every front. My inquisitive nature led to a deep curiosity concerning the validity of God. The seemingly superficial and unfair biased judgments, as well as the double-standard rules and parameters that I had observed my entire life, were beginning to shape my core belief system. Tiny fissures began to splinter my young heart, thus providing the underpinning necessary to continue constructing massive walls of insecurity.

Growing up I knew my Daddy loved me and would never leave me, but the truth is he was never a huge presence in my life because he was always working. I loved this quality about my Dad. I thought all Daddies worked hard like mine. I used to rub my fingers across the callouses formed in his hands through the years, not knowing at the time what those callouses represented. I was incredibly blessed to have an earthly Father who was not selfish, and who always strived to provide financially for his family the best he could. Daddy dropped out of school at a young age, only completing the ninth grade. He had worked physically hard his entire life. His body bore the proof of his dedication and work ethic. I am sure he was tired and discouraged at times. Daddy was one of the most honest, diligent, and persevering men I have ever known. I think that is why it was hard for him when he was finally forced to retire. His identity was wrapped up in being a provider for his family. Outside of that role, he did not understand his identity. His sole purpose was his family, the reason he did anything he did. Because my Mom took the role of disciplinarian and spiritual leader, I did not understand that I did not have a God-designed relationship with my Dad, although I had a loving relationship with him.

It is important to distinguish the differences between those two types of relationships. To me this relational interaction was normal. My growing and developing mind figured that this was how all Moms and Dads were. Likewise, I grew up attending church never understanding that Jesus Christ desired a one-on-one, daily, and personal relationship with me. I did not understand He desired to be in all the moments of my life. I didn't understand that I could count on Him and go to Him for comfort, encouragement, answers, direction, and wisdom. I knew He loved me. I knew He cared for me. I knew He died for me. I had grown up hearing the words of God without those words having application attached to them. I honestly did not know what I was supposed to do with Bible other than bring it to church. It certainly was not alive and active in my life. Without life application the Gospel was not taking root. I had no concept of the transformative power that it held. Going to church meant you knew you were an awful sinner in need of saving. Being saved meant I wouldn't burn in a lake of fire for all eternity. I knew about God. I knew God was watching over me and providing for me because that's what Daddies do. That was the extent of my association with God though. I do not think you could call it anything other than an association. There was no authentic relationship. It wouldn't be until years later that I would begin to discover God's core design deposited within each of us that longs for connection with Him.

CHAPTER 5
THE BREEDING GROUND OF FEAR

When my family decided to leave the little Baptist church I had called home for my entire life, we became members of a little Pentecostal church in the same community. I guess you could unofficially, or perhaps officially, call me Bapticostal! Now, let me just say this – this conversion and extreme alteration to my religious foundation was spiritual whiplash. Eccentric and most unconventional compared to my previous upbringing, the energetic atmosphere was most effervescent. That's the only way I know how to describe it. For the awkward and socially unskilled little girl who had only known her spiritual heritage to be that of a quiet reserve and disciplined emotional restraint, these vibrant and charismatic expressions of worship took a period of adaption, to say the least. But, adapt we did.

    I have many wonderful memories at this little church, however, just like before, there were many moments of hurt and rejection as well. If we are all honest, we can see our entire lives laced with experiences that have opportunity to develop and stretch us. I love that God has used every moment, as He often does, as a channel for my life's purpose to flow out of. Over time, God has allowed me to embrace something Pastor Robert Morris at Gateway Church calls Holy forgetfulness. I still have the memories, but they no longer haunt me. They are no longer a driving force behind my actions.

Instead, they serve as a propeller to God's purpose for my life. God has taught me to keep my focus on Him alone because humanity will always fail me. Humanity can never satisfy my deepest longings for acceptance and connection. God never intended for me to obtain from "man" that which only He can give. God alone has my best interest at heart, always going before me to clear the path and shine a light into darkness. Even in the valley of the shadow of death, I am not alone - for if there is a shadow, that means there is also the presence of light. Furthermore, shadows always loom and appear to be larger than they actually are. The light will always overpower the shadows of life.

Growing up I always had a deep longing to be heard and understood. The very thought of being dismissed or misunderstood would crush my spirit. Although I desired to remain invisible, melting into the backdrop of life, a craving for relational acceptance I saw others enjoying gnawed at my insides. This is because God designed us to live within the context of community. We are wired for connection. This longing for a relationship with others is engraved upon our hearts. Humanity is designed to perfectly fit together like the pieces of a puzzle, forming a much larger picture than we could ever accomplish on our own.

I have been able to trace the genesis of my insecurity and innate sense of rejection genetically as far back as my grandmother's childhood in the early 1930s. There is not a single doubt within my mind that the genetic coding runs deeper, but I have only been able to dig so deep at this time. Digging is an interesting term. Usually when we are digging it is because there is something valuable to be found beneath the surface; a treasure. We find throughout history that extraction is one of the most common reasons for digging. Understanding our heritage and history enables us to understand more fully our current situations and conditions. This in turn can be a tool of immense value, a great treasure to possess. Digging into our heritage to unearth our lineage helps us discover the truth of our ancestry, enabling us to settle our yesterdays once and for all. It empowers us to move forward into the life we were created and designed to live. Understanding our heritage is critical in discovering and breaking generational bondages, as well as in understanding why we are the way we are; why we do the things we do, or why we act in response to triggers the way we do. Understanding our past equips us to build a foundation for future generations that will allow them, as well as us, to be free from past addictions, bondages, and oppressions. The buck truly can stop with us! We can stop the perpetuating blame game. To suppress our heritage is to defeat our future before it ever happens. You cannot move forward by erasing or ignoring the past. To disregard our past is to discount the power of God and His authority to move on our behalf. Our heritage is valuable and worth digging for. We cannot ever hope to know who we are and live a life of freedom if we have no idea or concept of where we came from. Healthy and vibrant lives are not developed by wiping out and ignoring the past.

One thing I was certain of was this – the fear, insecurity, and uncertainty inside of me had been ingrained into the very fiber of my being from the womb. This fetal encrypting was not one I desired or even understood. My need to be heard, seen, and understood was a perplexing position to be in because I almost always felt uncomfortable with all eyes on me. It was a constant battle raging in my mind. Like my Dad, I have the ability to command attention, yet I nearly always search for ways to disappear into the background. A good example of this playing out current day would be my taking the entrance to our church on two wheels, with just enough time to rush in and find my seat as the intro-video to worship begins. This would safeguard me against lengthy conversations with people before service. Sitting close to the back exit allows me to grab my belongings and be out the door before anyone has an opportunity to fully engage with me. This has gotten much better as I have grown spiritually and matured in Christ, allowing Him to heal the deep and untouched recesses of my heart.

However, as a young teenager and adult, the struggle within was real y'all. The uncomfortable feelings that would wash over me when I knew others were looking at me were unbearable. I have felt the nauseating rush of an inferno combined with an iceberg charging me one too many times. You know what I am referring to – that cold sweat that makes you want to double over and disappear; makes you feel like you are going to hit the floor as your knees buckle beneath you.

Most of my childhood and adolescent memories are of those longing for acceptance and inclusion. There was a slight problem though. I wanted this acceptance and inclusion only on my own terms; therefore, I would purposely hold any glimmer of hope at arm's length. This would guarantee I would be able to maintain control of the situation and ultimately the outcome. I would be able to control others' perceived rejections by rejecting them first in advance of the alleged threat. If I was in control, I could always find an escape. I was never clever with impromptu or unrehearsed funny and witty comebacks, never proficient with ad libitum, and absolutely never the one with an illustrious sass and cool factor. I was more often unimpressive, almost always forgettable, and seemingly a throwaway, disposable, and invisible person in my own eyes. As I entered adolescence and young adulthood, I would find this waging internal war even more destructive and increasingly difficult to make sense of. Even if I managed to find entrance into a group, it was almost always short-lived. I would become physically ill if someone was at odds with me or did not like me. My reactive go-to was to airlift straight out of Dodge when the going got uncomfortable or tough. I was rather good at fleeing the scene – always good at playing dead. Paralysis, however, would not be a recommended coping mechanism I would endorse to anyone – not ever!

> Paralysis leads us to places *we wish we had never gone.* It robs us of purpose *and leads to an identity crisis.*

Spiritual paralysis is like the fog on the bathroom mirror after a long, hot, steamy shower. No sooner than you have wiped it clear, it fogs up again to the point you cannot see clearly. Just like that fog, spiritual paralysis prevents clear vision until someone opens the door and allows fresh air to come onto the scene.

I found solitude to be most comforting and accepting. It's a rather unresolved way to live that often left me unsettled. Yet, over time I grew to prefer my aloneness rather than connection and community. I developed an identity of being a" loner" marching to the beat of my very own drum. I always did things my way. The desire for connection became obsolete, buried, and stuffed down - barely detectable, yet it would become the great predictor and driving force behind most choices and decisions I made. Just thinking about how long I stayed trapped in this relentless cycle is hard to stomach. Satan loves to prey on our weaknesses and vulnerabilities, even in children. Satan never plays fair and he never only picks on those his own size. He preys on weak and vulnerable souls, kicking us when we are down to render us inoperable before we ever realize what is being done. His sole gain is in our total loss. He seeks to downplay our value and distort truth in hopes we will never discover we have a purpose. The only hope Satan has in "winning" is in taking us out. That is his goal. Knowing this truth gives you the home-field advantage.

    Unlike the church I had grown up in, our new home church had a youth group and I loved it. Finally, the deep longing for connection that continuously gnawed at my insides was receiving the spiritual nutrition and connection it craved. I looked forward to going to church any chance I got. I could not get enough of it. Ms. Ena Mae was a precious older lady who did her best to make sure all us kiddos knew we were loved by her. She wasn't perfect, she didn't hold any official titles or fancy degrees, and she was very unconventional, but she loved us bunch of wiry and unruly kids with a love bigger than her little body. We were her mission and purpose in life.

There was always something fun to do – like sleepovers and lock-ins, boating trips, shopping, makeovers, and going for walks. There was even a youth choir. I had hit the jackpot of my lifetime. As scratchy and rough as we were around the edges, we would sing our hearts clear out of our chests, with Ms. Ena Mae right down in front of us waving her hands so as to direct us vocally. Our little church seemed to enjoy our worship almost as much as we did. They always praised our efforts and allowed plenty of opportunities for us to glorify God through song and drama.

It was in this youth choir that I would experience my first rejections and judgments by my youth group peers. Let me preface this story by sharing this simple truth – we were all kids. We were all learning, growing, developing, and daily being transformed to reflect the nature and heart of God. None of us had it all together. I am certain others within the youth group have their own stories and revelations they could share about this passage and season of life. I do not believe any of my experiences were aimed at truly causing me intentional harm or discomfort. As often it is with teenagers, words were careless and actions were not very well thought out. The truth of the lyrics of the song I used to sing in the little Baptist church we attended, *"He's still working on me, to make me what I ought to be,"* rang true for all of us.

I loved singing. When I was 17 years old, I placed first runner-up in a state competition for our church denomination. I had chosen to play it safe in my song choice due to my insecurity. This was the sole reason I had not taken grand-prize, and thus traveling on to Nationals according to the judge's notes we received afterward. They knew I was capable of more than I gave that day. They were disappointed in my decision to take the easy road, and in turn I became disappointed in myself. If only they had known that simply being there on that stage was a huge feat for me. If only they had known I gave all I knew I had, because the remainder had yet to be developed and cultivated. In my 30s I was honored to be invited to serve as a vocal judge for the State of Illinois Teen Talent Competition as well. Additionally, I served as a Praise and Worship Leader in my local church in my 20s and 30s. I used to make the statement that I did not know if I could exist if I could not sing. Singing was my core identity (another flawed structure built on a rickety and unstable foundation) and the only thing I ever thought I was any good at (another huge lie of the enemy). Singing would eventually become an idol because I felt accepted by both God and others when I would sing. It checked all the boxes and allowed me to feel important, significant, connected, heard, and seen. I wrongly associated my worth and value with a talent and gift. If I did not receive verbal praise and accolades after I would sing, I felt like a failure. My performance became just that, a show in need of a response and a review - a performance in need of acceptance - instead of worship and heart-felt adoration to God. I never realized growing up that singing was a gift God had given me to display His glory and to sharpen my focus on His beauty, His splendor, His magnificence, and His grandeur. I used it as a mechanism for personal gain. Of course, I did not know that was what I was doing. My heart and mind could not comprehend the level of deception at the time that was being used to form weapons against me and within me.

I was always singing specials in church. In fact, I was always singing period. I have memories as a little child standing on the top of an old camper out behind our house, a stick or hairbrush as my microphone, with the skies, scorpions, ants, and trees as my audience, singing my heart out without a care in the world. That competition I mentioned earlier, well, I was so over-the-top excited at my accomplishments that I carried my ridiculously oversized trophy into the local Piggly Wiggly where I worked to show it off that night. Yes, true story. I am sitting here shaking my head at myself as I type this out, as I still feel slightly embarrassed at the silliness of it all.

Now, back to our original story. Ms. Ena Mae was not a professional musician and never assigned song parts based on a person's talent, ability, or capacity to deliver. Every time a new song was introduced, she would simply ask everyone - all at once - who wanted to sing the solo parts. It was always on a volunteer basis. She could not have cared any less if someone could sing or not, or if it was even in a key that was good for their voice (we used soundtracks). If someone wanted to sing, they were allowed to. End of discussion. There were times others would raise their hands, however, this was usually not the case. After a period of time waiting out the hemming and hawing around, I would raise my hand. That is when the commentary would begin, *"but you always sing the solos, you need to let someone else have a chance."* Of course, others rarely volunteered and Ms. Ena Mae never stopped the criticism. This went on for a number of years. I eventually came to a place where I lost interest and began to hold back.

Ms. Ena Mae's refrain was simple - *do good, do not kiss frogs, and God has a plan for you*. Oddly enough, there was plenty of truth mixed into her well-hearted sentiment. There was also just enough deception to keep a young girl who was unsteady in her faith from recognizing the whole truth.

My brother was never as active in the youth group as I was. He was always busy with his buddies, mud-riding and getting into no-good trouble as usual. At church he always sat on the back row cutting up with the other boys. No worries, he would laugh reading this because he knows it was true. He was known by several alias names, all of which deserve to be monogrammed onto a shirt or mug for their brilliant marketing value, and of course, because we monogram everything in the South!

Jake the Snake
Hot Lips Harris
Trouble Maker

Jake often pulled me into his shenanigans. Being the compliant little sister, I was always happy to oblige. Like the time he decided to chop off half my hair when our babysitter had enjoyed a long night of partying and fell asleep on the couch; a tiny little detail unbeknownst to my Mother. Or, like the time he decided to take me for a walk down the side of a main highway when I was around two years old. Or, like the time he unwrapped his Christmas

Nikes each morning after Mom left for work so he could wear them to school. Each afternoon he would clean them up with a wet rag, carefully place them back into the box and slide them back into the wrapping paper, sealing them with clear tape. He would look at me out of the corner of his eye every morning as I looked on. I knew what that glare meant. I knew I would face his wrath if I tattled on him. We finally told Momma this story when we were well into adulthood and we knew she could not possibly spank us. One year during the Powder Puff Football game, my brother mooned the entire football stadium from the field. I was completely mortified. I am pretty sure it was as much a surprise to him as it was to the rest of us. The guys were the cheerleaders and were running from side to side pulling stunts and tricks on the other team. During one of those stunts his sweatpants got jerked clear down to his ankles. Although it had not been intentional, I still could not help but dive under the mountain of coats piled up beside me and my friends. There was also the time my brother tied a rope around my waist and proceeded to attempt pulling me up a tree - by my waist y'all. I couldn't climb the tree because my arm was in a cast - one of those old-school heavy plaster cast that went nearly up to my shoulder - due to another shenanigan of his. We laugh to this day about my broken arm because I am positively certain it was planned mutiny by him and our buddy, Anthony, although they both deny all facts presented. The day I came into the kitchen crying with an arm that hung in a "u" shape is the day I saw my Mom turn three shades of green. Back to the tree story - there I was, compliant as ever, fully trusting in my big brother, with a rope tied around my little waist. Thankfully my Mom looked out the kitchen window in time to rescue me from yet another adventure gone wrong.

This was the legacy I followed in school as well. By the time high school rolled around, teachers had already pre-judged and pre-labeled me as "Jake's little sister." Their eyes were already rolling into the back of their heads at just seeing my name on the roll call. It was an uphill climb from the beginning. It would only be after handing in a well-written essay that one teacher would exclaim, *"I had you wrong Miss Valerie, I thought you were going to be just like your brother."* There would be many times I would have to prove my worthiness of their acceptance and approval. This strengthened the platform of my already developing people-pleasing patterns, patterns born on the breeding ground of fear and rejection because I longed for the teachers to like me and accept me. I wanted to be treated how I perceived the other students were being treated. I wanted to prove that I was a good person, a worthy person.

The Great Reversal

One Saturday our youth group had planned a trip to Six Flags. I had been beyond excited about this trip for months on end. There had never been a lot of excess money for annual vacations when we were growing up, so this trip was a rarity and something I had been looking forward to. We had all worked hard the entire year to raise the money for everyone to go. We held rock-a-thons, walk-a-thons, car washes, sold BBQ and hamburger lunches, sold candy bars (which I may or may not have eaten more than I sold), and collected donations for a huge church yard sale. My brother had not lifted a single finger to help with any of the fundraising efforts. The morning of the trip my brother decided to ride with us to the church. This was unusual as Jake didn't often ride anywhere with the family – mostly because he would rather have died than be seen with us in public. (Don't worry – once again, he would admit this.) Most likely Mom had promised him that she would stop in town for something he wanted as a bribe. Even today, Jake will tell you that his compliance in those days usually had personal gain attached to it. When we arrived at the church with only a few minutes to spare (I suppose I come by it naturally), everyone jumped into the van and I was the last one to try and find a seat. This was my longing to be included yet holding any chance of inclusion at arm's length in full view. Much to my disappointment everyone said there was no more room. This must be how Mary and Joseph felt as they were told the same exact thing. My brother was spotted still sitting in the car and before I knew what was happening, everyone was begging for him to come along. In my mind I was screaming, **NO!** – but of course, my silent theatrics were of little help. Everyone assured him there was room and plenty of money to cover the ticket. After convincing him to tag along, they made room for him in the church van, but there I was – still standing outside of the church van looking on. Of course, true to my nature, I disappeared into the backdrop and did not speak up for myself. Why would I have wanted to when they clearly did not want me to ride with them to begin with. They all rode together to Six Flags that day while I rode alone, by myself, with two adult chaperones. What surprises me to this day is that not a single adult in my life took notice and spoke up for me. No one stepped up and said they would ride with me either. The rejection I felt that day was immense, and continued to fortify the pent-up worst beliefs I already suspected were true about me. The belief that I was nothing, a nobody, and no one enjoyed my company. Perhaps it was my clothes. The fortune cookie from the Chinese restaurant must have been correct when it said that fashion made me beautiful. Or maybe I was ugly and fat. Maybe I did not know how to engage and talk with others. Again, all lies that I added to my existing and ever-expanding identity crisis portfolio.

As an adult, God has shown me two distinct lessons from this experience that across a span of two and half decades had deceptively shaped and formed my opinion of myself – a deception that became the gold standard of measurement for which I assessed my value and worth. Many times, this great deception would mislead and misguide me down paths God never intended me to go.

First, even when I am rejected by those with whom I should feel most accepted, He still longs to be in my company. This is an important truth essential to living a life of freedom. Jesus desires to be in an authentic and intimate relationship with me. Not only that, but He also takes great joy in doing so. It is never a chore to Him. It is not a routine. It is not an imposition. It is never out of duty. God has taken immense pleasure in His creation, me! In His presence, there is always room for me. God is not like a man who is capable of lies. His very essence cannot permit such. God is not deficient or lacking in any way. He is fully complete in and of Himself, possessing the power and the absolute authority to bring fulfillment to His word - the way, the truth, and the life! Jesus is not merely tolerating my existence for the sake of saving face or keeping with obligations. He genuinely delights in every single moment I come to sit at the foot of the cross. He looks forward to it.

It is clear throughout Scripture that it was God's idea and desire to establish a relationship between human beings and Himself through redemption and restoration found at the Cross. This love story filled the gap and bridged the aperture separating God from His beloved creation. From the beginning, God had a plan for humanity. We were created in His image to reflect Him, His nature, and His very heart. Satan has stopped short of nothing to distort and adulterate this simple, beautiful truth.

This is the written account of the descendants of Adam. When God created human beings, he made them to be like himself. Genesis 5:1 NLT

We, though, are going to love—love and be loved. First, we were loved, now we love. He loved us first.
1 John 4:19 The Message Translation (MSG)

There is a natural and abundant blessing that marks my life when I choose to partake in this divine exchange. When I choose relationship with others over seclusion, accessibility over unapproachability, and presence over distancing myself - it is in these moments that my heart is synchronized into the perfect unforced rhythms of His grace, love, and mercy talked about in Matthew 11. In all my working and striving for the Six Flags trip, I adopted a deeply embedded, and yet extremely flawed belief that I was included, chosen, special, and accepted because of how hard I had contributed to the overall goal. I had proven myself as a worthy team member. I loved the feeling of acceptance and inclusion. However, In God's currency, there is nothing I can do to buy His inclusion, acceptance, and blessing. There is nothing I can do to earn it. It is a gift He alone desires to give to me. There are no exceptions to God's unfailing love. In choosing to continually prove my own self-worth, I devalued the very worth of my life as God's creation. I can never and will never be able to do enough to earn God's favor, presence, love, and acceptance of me. It just simply is – if I have the courage to possess it and to believe it.

    Because we live in a performance-based culture that teaches a concept contrary to this belief, it is easy to see how so many conclude that personal effort equals recompense and return. Performance-based thinking undermines the truth of God's nature and screams that we do not think God is big enough to be who He says He is. If I believe I will only be happy if _____ (You fill in the blank) happens, then not only have I made whatever is in the blank an idol, but I have also discounted God's ability and authority in my life. I cannot justify myself. I cannot cleanse myself. I cannot make myself worthy. I cannot control other's acceptance of me because things and people will ever be able to satisfy my deepest longings.

But because of his great love for us, God, who is rich in mercy, made us alive with Christ even when we were dead in transgressions—it is by grace you have been saved. And God raised us up with Christ and seated us with him in the heavenly realms in Christ Jesus, in order that in the coming ages he might show the incomparable riches of his grace, expressed in his kindness to us in Christ Jesus. For it is by grace you have been saved, through faith—and this is not from yourselves, it is the gift of God—not by works, so that no one can boast. For we are God's handiwork, created in Christ Jesus to do good works, which God prepared in advance for us to do. Ephesians 2: 4-10 NIV

Second, even in my hurt and pain, there was always a bigger picture at play. It was never just about me. I recently saw an image on social media of a man lying on his stomach trying to hold onto the arm of a lady who had fallen off the side of a cliff. In a crevasse in the rock, there was a snake. The woman could not understand why the man would not pull her up faster to prevent the snake from biting her. She was screaming in terror and begging for him to move faster. What she could not see was the boulder that had crushed his back and the blood rolling down his body. Holding onto her hand was all he was able to do.

This visual is a perfect picture of our lives sometimes. **Focusing solely on our own pain and situations will cripple our ability to be empathetic, as well as our ability to see beyond ourselves.** Satan was trying to keep my brother from the connection found in community. My brother needed to feel included that day. My brother has always suffered from Bipolar Disorder, although it went undiagnosed until early adulthood. The extreme highs and lows often left him feeling isolated, dejected, and unworthy. This would often lead to self-preservation in the forms of hurtful and often hateful attitudes and disruptive behaviors. The emotional swings also made steady and healthy relationships very difficult, if not near impossible, for him. All I could see was how he did not put forth any effort and yet, he was still doted over. I felt invisible. I imagine however, my brother had felt invisible for a very long time. He is also God's creation and God wanted to love on him that day and remind him he was not abandoned or deserted.

God wanted him to feel chosen too. I can see that now, but then – not so much. God has shown me through this unveiling of truth that recognizing the bigger picture does not minimize my pain in the smaller picture in any way. He is God and I am not. I must trust His nature when I cannot see His hands; when I feel abandoned and alone.

God's kingdom is like an estate manager who went out early in the morning to hire workers for his vineyard. They agreed on a wage of a dollar a day, and went to work. Later, about nine o'clock, the manager saw some other men hanging around the town square unemployed. He told them to go to work in his vineyard and he would pay them a fair wage. They went. He did the same thing at noon, and again at three o'clock. At five o'clock he went back and found still others standing around. He said, Why are you standing around all day doing nothing? They said, Because no one hired us. He told them to go to work in his vineyard. When the day's work was over, the owner of the vineyard instructed his foreman, call the workers in and pay them their wages. Start with the last hired and go on to the first. Those hired at five o'clock came up and were each given a dollar. When those who were hired first saw that, they assumed they would get far more. But they got the same, each of them one dollar. Taking the dollar, they groused angrily to the manager, these last workers put in only one easy hour, and you just made them equal to us, who slaved all day under a scorching sun. He replied to the one speaking for the rest, Friend, I haven't been unfair. We agreed on the wage of a dollar, didn't we? So, take it and go. I decided to give to the one who came last the same as you. Can't I do what I want with my own money? Are you going to get stingy because I am generous? Here it is again, the Great Reversal: many of the first ending up last, and the last first. Matthew 20: 1-16 The Message Translation (MSG)

How God chooses to work and distribute is not necessarily the way I would, and that is no doubt for the best! I promise you! We are told in Scripture that God's ways and thoughts are higher than ours. We cannot possibly see the bigger picture at play, but usually knowing this will not stop us from becoming frustrated and disheartened with our situation. In an authentic relationship with God, we will eventually come to a crossroads in life that will require us to come up to a higher elevation; to a higher vantage point. It is a higher frame of mind and perspective focused on others and not on self. We will be challenged to advance past enemy lines. We will be dared to believe for greater things. We will be confronted with truth that will demand our response; a truth that will demand our surrender. God's love compels us to love others. Always has and always will. That is the economy of God's Kingdom.

I believe the way God defines rewards here on earth is vastly different from the way we define it. I believed that because I had worked and proven myself, I should be rewarded with a wonderful experience, acceptance, and acknowledgment from others - as well as accolades and "atta-girl" pats on the back. This response is what seemed right in my economy. I also believed that my brother, who had not made any effort, did not deserve the trip or the time spent with others. He was taking the spot that should have been mine in the van. And there we have it guys – pure jealousy, entitlement, self-righteousness, arrogance, smugness, and pride on full display! It is not a very pretty sight at all.

Jesus never disaffirmed my pain of feeling rejected and invisible that day. He did not shun or abandon me in my despondency. He did, however, long for me to see the bigger picture. He longed for me to see something more than my own point of view. He wanted me to grow, stretch, and learn so my roots could grow deep and my soul could become nourished and healthy – enabling me to live a life of healing, peace, and freedom. No amount of doing, working, and striving makes any difference to God. God sees us all as equals. We all get equal access to forgiveness, grace, love, and mercy when we turn our hearts toward Him. Thank God we do not get what we deserve and what truth declares as "fair." I was being called to a place of vulnerability that would require me to enter a partnership with God. This partnership would only be possible if I chose to surrender all the fractured parts of my heart. This partnership would involve a sacrifice of my feelings on the altar of His purpose and plan. This brave surrender gave me a new perspective and understanding of peace I had never known before. It has been the complete surrender of the secret hurts and pains I held onto for so long that led me to finally understand what "Let Go and Let God" really meant.

My friend, God longs to heal you as well. Sometimes our healing will be a gentle washing of our heart, like a breath of fresh air that breathes new life into our lungs. Other times God will take us on a journey that allows us to have a different viewpoint of the situation. Sometimes God desires to bring a different perspective to the table, while other times He will lovingly correct our broken viewfinder. Photographers use a viewfinder to help them compose and focus a picture. The viewfinder gives the photographer the ability to see in advance what will be captured in the photograph later. A viewfinder gives the photographer an advantage that others do not have. If the viewfinder is broken or not working correctly, it will impact the overall quality of the end product. It is much like an airplane pilot flying blind. If our ability to navigate has been congested by everything life has thrown our way, causing us to view our day-to-day life through a lens of hurt and pain, we will be unable to see God's hands at work. We must stop, take a deep breath, and say, *"Okay God, I cannot do this on my own. What are you wanting to show me? I need you to help me see."* God can only do this for us though if we allow Him to. There is a song I love by a group called *Selah*. The song simply says, *God will take away your pain if you'll choose to let it go.* Let me challenge you today to let it all go. Choose to let your hurt and pain go. Choose to allow God to repair your viewfinder. Watch what God can do with daring faith and courageous determination like this!

CHAPTER 6
MORNING CUPS OF JOY

Most school mornings were nigh on the verge of WWIII when my children were younger. It was always rush, Rush, and then **RUSH** some more from the moment my eyes opened and my feet hit the ground. The tone was stressed and the tone was loud! This was an exact repeat of how most mornings were in my home growing up as well. Mom was not a morning person and she always struggled to wake up on time, despite the use of an alarm clock. We now know this was because she had undiagnosed sleep apnea that prevented her from getting the consistent good quality of sleep her body was in desperate need of. Because Mom always slept until the last minute, she was on edge trying to get out of the door in time to make it to work. I'm sure her daily hunt for makeup I had borrowed didn't help matters much either. Don't get me wrong, Momma was wonderful – but, she was far from being a chipper morning person. There were a lot of short-tempered mornings challenged by raging teenage hormones made worse by her yelling to get a point across. I'm not sure why we often think being loud makes us more effective and impactful. We've all done it a time or two – I'm guilty as charged. In those days, most mornings my feeble attempt at getting myself ready included a messy bun on top of my head – mind you this was before messy buns were cool. My messy buns never looked cool and sexy like the pictures you see on social media or in magazines either. At best, I always looked more like I had been chased by wild animals for the entire night before. Maybe I was part of the movement that brought them into style. Yes, I think I will stick with that version of my story.

I recall one morning that will forever be a vivid memory in my catalogue of things I wish I could permanently press delete on. I came into consciousness to find that it was seven minutes before the bus was scheduled to run. At that time, I was living paycheck to paycheck with less than $20 to my name and an entire week until the next payday. Extra gas money to run my son across town to the specialized school he was attending at the time was not in the budget. Also, he had already missed far too many days so skipping school that day was not an option, although the thought did briefly enter my mind. As panic set in, I jumped out of the bed and took off running while my feet were still apparently asleep. They had not received the message that it was time to move. I found myself suspended in the air as my body flew through the living room aimed toward my son's room. At one point I am certain my feet flew over my head. Apparently my numb and groggy legs slipped somewhere along the way and had gone airborne, my forehead greeting the wall with a morning how-do-you-do. This left a nice shiner that hung around for a few weeks. Ouch! I dented the sheetrock wall that morning with my forehead. Now I only had six minutes to get my son awake, dressed, and out the door onto the bus.

There was not a bone in my son's body that knew what the word "hurry" actually meant. He seemed to move along at the same slow pace despite my colorful and hyper script of encouragement. Amazingly I managed to accomplish this seemingly impossible task, all while throwing a Pop-Tart up the stairs to him as he made his way to his seat. I thanked God this was not a morning he chose to buck the system. Probably because he wasn't awake enough to have a consciousness about what he was being told to do. This is a rather extreme story that is, in hindsight, extremely comical.

How I started that day set the tone for the remainder of the day. I was stressed out. Nothing went right. My son was stressed out. I was snappy with everyone I encountered. I was mad that we had to eat Ramen Noodles, yet again, for dinner. Didn't God understand that carbs were not my friend? Imagine if I had started that morning with a simple shift. Even though I was severely running behind I could have opened my eyes and thanked God for another day and invited Him into my day – all of 30 seconds y'all. Six and half minutes later, once my son was on the bus, and after grabbing a cup of coffee, I could have continued that conversation with God. But I did not. Why? It was not my habit.

Perhaps this story will be a bit more relatable. My husband and I wake up very early. I do not think the roosters are even awake at 3:00 am. My morning routine is relatively the same every single day. My goals are to caffeinate myself (a detail of grave importance), then cook and pack his breakfast, mid-morning snack, lunch, and coffee for the road. Once finished, I then proceed to lay out his daily vitamins and immunity boosting supplements, along with his keys, wallet, and his ball cap. Although I am an early morning person, sometimes those early morning to-dos are not without their challenges. I cannot tell you how many times I have made coffee without coffee grounds in the pot. I excel in brewing hot water. A simple morning cup of joy brings enlightenment and clarity to my day, waking up my senses and setting me on a path to success. Once I get Tommy all packed up, I will make the bed and piddle until he has left for work. At that point, I usually fix (yes, fix is a word comparable to the word prepare where I come from – ha!) the second cup of glorious morning joy and make my way to the living room for some alone time with God. I enjoy my quiet mornings and time with God, and my intentions are the best. Much healing, growth, and infusion of wisdom has come from those moments with God in the secret place. Destinies are designed and dreams are conceived in the secret place. Marching orders are handed out in the secret place. But, if I am going to be honest with you, there have been many a morning that I have become distracted and had to reel myself back in.

It's not hard for me to become distracted. I must be intentional. Some mornings I find myself strategizing over the best ways to get the most accomplished. If I go ahead and throw a load of laundry in, finish loading the dishwasher and turn it on, make the bed, and get the food prep going, then I can sit down and have my time alone with God while all that is simultaneously going on. What a great use of time management that deserves an "atta-girl." After all, God loves when we steward everything well, and that must include our time. Perfection! Well, sort of. In one fell swoop, I have justified the best use of time instead of trusting the creator of time itself. The problem when I do this – is I have made God a part of my to-do list that I simply check off, instead of making God the creator of my entire day; instead of starting my day in recognition and adoration of Him. Sound familiar? I bet if we are all honest with ourselves, we can identify areas such as this that need a bit of tidying up.

It is easy to get off course. I am a list maker of all list makers. My to-do list is always a mile long and never-ending. In fact, my to-do list has its very own secondary to-do list – an overflow spiral notebook in which I can expand on the task I need to accomplish for the day. If I do something not on my to-do list, I will add it for the pleasure and feeling of accomplishment that comes when I cross it off. I am in need of an intervention! I can always find something to do and there is always work to be done. I even schedule personal phone calls and exercise time. Perhaps mostly so I won't forget them, but still the same - they find their way to my list. I have learned to relax a bit as I've gotten older though. The season of perimenopause that has made its unwelcome entrance has made becoming less rigid a necessity. When I get to the end of my day and the list is not complete, I have learned (and am still learning) to let it go instead of viewing myself as a failure. It will be there at the beginning of the next day. I have pre-decided to stop allowing my unrealistic expectations of myself to run rampant in my mind. I have found that being intentional and focused helps. I have also learned that identifying the excessiveness and non-essentials in my life - and, clearing them out - is critical. Letting go of what I want to accomplish right now to grab ahold of what I want most is the driving force that helps keep me focused. Implementing guardrails helps insure I stay on the path I desire most of all. Instead of getting derailed by all life's distractions, deciding in advance to ignore the notifications on the tablet and phone will make it easy when I am presented with that choice. When I hear a ding, or when I see a red dot, I immediately remember that I have already chosen the better path - to delay my response. The choice is simple. Better yet is to turn off the volume on the phone until later in the morning. In choosing to prioritize the purpose and mission of my life over what seems practical to me, I am choosing principles based on the truth of God's word that will endorse and make way for hope and promise to unfold.

God has given each of us the gift of choice. When we choose something, we are picking it by preference over all the other choices that might be available to us. Our choices give way to the priorities and motivations living inside of us, even when those choices contradict the words we are speaking. Although our words are incredibly powerful and impactful, we must not forget that our actions have their own voice, or lack thereof. We are to be doers, not just hearers, and not just speakers. Doers. That means that truth must be applied and implemented to bring about true heart transformation. The life we are living is a result of the choices and decisions we have made, whether those choices are for the good or the bad. The choices and disciplines we practice in seclusion with God will set the tone for our days and our lives. The friends we choose to hang around with consistently will determine the curvature, latitude, and scope of our lives. If we choose to eat Pop-Tarts, Doritos, and Oreos every day, we will reap a harvest of an ever-expanding waistline, as well as the inevitable health issues that accompany it as a result. The altered tone of our day is pre-set if we choose to start our mornings by flipping on the news and scrolling through social media first instead of in acknowledgment to and gratefulness for the Great I Am.

Every day we wake up we are presented with an opportunity that is ours for the taking. Every day we can make choices that will position us for a lifetime of possibilities, or that will frame out a lifetime of heartache and self-imposed trials. Choosing to step outside of what makes sense to us, outside of what seems practicable to us, cultivates space for God to move. Stepping into what is possible through a partnership with God will allow us to experience an entirely different way He intended for us to live our lives. We were never designed to make our choices based on demands, pressures, and busyness. Those things were never meant to rule or motivate us. Rather, our choices should reflect the purpose He has ordained for our lives. This purpose is outlined in the truths found within the Scriptures. As we start each day with God, let us pour ourselves a morning cup of joy. Let us begin by asking for the Holy Spirit to guide our every step. Our loving Heavenly Father has hopes and plans for us - hopes and plans for a future filled with promise in which all things are possible. He can do exceedingly far above anything we could ever think, imagine, or think to imagine!

He is extending to us the invitation to walk in communion with Him in a perfect rhythm of grace.

I love this translation of Jeremiah 29:11. God offers to us the opportunity, but it is our choice to reach out and embrace it. He does not force it on us.

For I know full well the plans I have for you, plans for your welfare and not for your misfortune, plans that will offer you a future filled with hope. Jeremiah 29:11 NCB

He knows full well, in other words – the plans He has for us are not even comparable to anything we could possibly imagine. There is no doubt if you are a parent, you know this desire you have for your children. We deeply long for our children to learn from our mistakes, exploits, knowledge, and experiences so they can avoid the same bumps that tripped us up in life. We desperately long to shelter and protect our children from anything that could bring them harm. We want them to have the best life. An abundant life. A prosperous life. We hate to see them hurt and suffer. The stories I share about our son Eli throughout this book are a great example of this very sentiment. At the end of the day, we must take to heart that we cannot force our children to listen and apply all that we are training them in. Just as God our Father gives us a choice to choose a life of purpose and promise, our children have a choice as well.

The ripple effect of the choices we each make has an impact far greater reaching than we could ever imagine. Our choices will always have a direct impact on others around us. We have learned that it is wise to allow margin for someone else's error in life, much like a buffer or taking precautionary measures. My husband and I love to ride our Harley on the Tail of the Dragon in North Carolina. The 318 curves in the 11-mile winding mountain road are packed full of adventurous, daring, and blind-faith moments. It is always wise to allow for the error of someone else's choice or else you could find yourself up close and personal with someone rounding a curve in your lane going double or triple the speed limit. If this happens you might also find your motorcycle or car parts hanging from the Tree of Shame located at the end of The Tail of the Dragon. Unfortunately, not all survive the collisions that occur on this road.

The choices we make one hundred percent determine the person we will become. They will lay the foundation for future generations yet to be born. The enemy of our souls hopes we will never recognize the vast truth and impact this one little nugget holds. Choosing wisely to live a life anchored by hope and rooted in truth will expose the lies of Satan. This truth is whispered into our souls, but culture shouts – *You do you! Do what makes you feel good. If others don't like it, find a different tribe.* We live in a society that chooses to cancel one another every single time there is a disagreement on anything. Our choices do matter. They matter for us. They matter for our families. They matter for our communities. They matter for our nation. Choosing morning cups of joy will help us recognize lies as we filter them through the lens of truth. Truth when applied and put into action brings forth freedom and peace.

CHAPTER 7
OUR UGLY DOESN'T SCARE GOD

What happens when you find yourself in a place that requires you to forgive your child? I am not talking about forgiving them for lifting that pack of gum from the store, although that is not right and should be dealt with. I am not talking about forgiving your daughter for taking your eyeliner without asking, once again (Sorry Momma). I am not talking about forgiving your child for slamming their bedroom door. Those infractions are relatively easy to forgive and move on. I am talking about deep forgiveness for actions that have destroyed others. A deep forgiveness for the unsettling of multiple families; for the destruction of hopes and dreams. Forgiveness that would require going against every grain of your being. A forgiveness that would seem irrational to one's unredeemed state of mind.

This is a story about God's unfailing strength – a story about God's incredible, radical, and most generous kindness and love extended to a daughter who was breaking. It is a story about a daughter of a King who made a choice and decision in the fall of 2019, a choice she'd never found courage to make before. This one decision would change everything, forever. The ripple effect of her decision impacted her family in healthy ways as they have watched her learn to walk this grace road - a road she did not choose herself. They watched as she chose to keep moving forward, discovering an authentic love in the devotion of a Father who never called her to walk in perfection. He simply called her to walk, placing one foot in front of the other, and trusting Him along the way. They watched as she learned to rest in His unforced rhythms of grace. Her choice to trust God during great difficulty sent out a shockwave to those around her.

Me. I am that daughter. This is my story and how I was influencing lives with my choices even when I could not see a way through my pain. Others saw that I kept moving forward and trusting God, even when reality collided with my own hopes and dreams; even when I felt I could not take another step. I have learned to let go of my hopes and dreams to embrace God's plan - a plan I would have never chosen and a plan that is still hard to reckon with, still hard to moderate, and still hard to calculate to this day. Despite its difficulty, I chose to rewrite the narrative Satan was trying to destroy our family with. I did this through surrender and trust. It was not easy. It did not feel good. Most days it was downright ugly. However, I chose to flip the script. I chose to embrace the undeniable truth that my ability to comprehend and understand may never calculate or fully compute. It may never make sense and never add up. And you know what? It's okay. It is okay because the truth of the matter is, it does not have to make sense. Learning to find a place of resolve was part of my healing journey that taught me how to persevere. This was a journey that would require tenacity, stubbornness, and persistence in my pursuit of freedom and peace; in my pursuit of becoming COMPLETELY His!

There would be many moments in this journey that would demand my walking a Red Sea Road to freedom. Roads that would often require deep reflection, Holy revival of dead bones, spiritual renewal of my innermost spaces, and physical recovery as He gently remade what was into His newness.

I did not know it was possible to love someone so much you would give your life up for them, while at the same time needing to extend unfathomable forgiveness and grace to them. Isn't this a perfect picture of the cross?

It was a morning like most others, nothing extraordinarily different or remarkable to note. The sun was just beginning to peek and I could see it beginning to shed light through my wall of kitchen windows. We are blessed to live in a peaceful and beautiful small town located just outside of Gadsden, Alabama. Our incredible scenic views offer a safe-haven and refuge from the crazed, raving demands of our life. We feel exceedingly fortunate to live where we live. The peacefulness we experience is an absolute treasure. We have amazing neighbors we are blessed to call friends. We have the most beautiful sunrises and sunsets not distorted by distractions of sirens and horns; a glimpse of God's extraordinary canvas and artwork most every day. I love to hear the roosters crowing from across the field, demanding we all stand up and take notice of their dominance. Many mornings in the spring and fall I try to make it a point to sit on the back porch, sipping on my third round of coffee (by that time) and watching, or rather listening to the world wake up while the birds sing their beautiful melodies. Choosing to cherish these moments, and not overlook their splendor and impact, has held deep healing and immense value for my heart during this season of life.

    This particular morning my husband had already left for work and I was unloading dishes from the dishwasher when I first heard a voice. The voice. His voice. Impossible to mistake, I recognized this voice immediately. It was impossible to ignore. Although it wasn't audible it demanded I stop and take notice. The Holy Spirit whispered,

"Tragedy will come, do not fear."

    I remember it like it was yesterday. I will never forget those words. I stopped what I was doing, frozen in the moment. There had only been a few other times in my life I had so distinctively and undeniably heard the voice of God this forcefully and firmly. I knew in an instance what was being spoken would take place.

The Holy Spirit whispered it to my spirit many times that day, as He would continue to do over the course of the next several months. I could not understand what it was or why, but I knew God was preparing me. I didn't like the stinging fact that was gnawing at me and found myself frequently questioning God, wanting to know what **IT** was. How could God speak to me in such vagueness!? It was driving me crazy. A few months passed and the daily whispers began to fade away. I cannot recall specifically when they actually stopped. I tucked the word away in the back of my heart and mind, and life went on. Although for months I did not consciously think about it, I also never completely forgot about it.

One mid-November afternoon, as I stood once again unloading the dishwasher, I heard the same whisper. What is it about me and the dishwasher? Maybe that is the only time my mind isn't running a grueling marathon. The familiar and gentle reminder that seemed to be preparing me as it whispered, *"Tragedy will come, do not fear,"* once again swept over my spirit. Ever commanding as the first time, with a bit more assertion, there was no mistake. It would be that evening that I would receive the news that would forever change our lives. Nothing in our world would ever be the same. How could it be? It was incomprehensible to imagine and immediately my heart filled with pain, disbelief, horror, anger, denial, and yes – even fear. I could not wrap my head around the news and initially thought it couldn't possibly be true. My husband and I both struggled with unbelief, seeking validation of its truth. But I simply knew. I knew what my heart wasn't ready to acknowledge was the truth because God, in His grace, had already begun to prepare me months before. That preparedness didn't remove the initial shockwave and sting, but it did help me hold on to hope.

Raising Eli had NEVER been "easy," as if raising any child is. Any budding hopes that had been buried deep within me shattered into a million fragmented pieces that November evening. Have you ever had a moment like this? A moment in which every ounce of grit you had inside of you belted out,

No! It shouldn't be this way!
This cannot be happening.
This cannot be true.
This cannot be my life.
It's so unfair God.
Haven't we already been through enough, God?

Life was not ever supposed to be this way, you know? My life. My son's life. Our family's lives. This was not the dream. This was not the hopes I had pinned up within my heart. This was not my plan. My plan and my hopes looked vastly different than this black hole of anguish and heartache staring back at us. I did not want to hear Jeremiah 29:11. I did not want to hear any Scripture for that matter. I was crumbling under the weight and these new findings were unraveling me at the seams. I found it difficult to sleep. I woke up with tears immediately in my eyes, as if my soul had been crying subconsciously while I tried to sleep. The roller coaster of emotions that would flood my body over the course of the months that followed was mostly indescribable and excruciatingly painful. Clothed in disbelief I lived completely numb, while at the same time having a hyper-sensitivity to life itself. I was fragile. I was despondent. I was beyond discouraged. I was brokenhearted in every sense of the way. I did not want anyone to know, yet I knew life wasn't meant to be lived in isolation. We are designed to live within the context of community with others. It is with others we find comfort, strength, and encouragement. I was fearful of what others would think if they knew though. How could I ever be open and honest about something like this? So, I did what every good little church girl does. I did what my upbringing in church had taught me - I put on my mask when I was around others. I never took it off.

For weeks I could not leave the house because I cried non-stop at pretty much everything. I could not hold a conversation with anyone, so I ignored phone calls, text messages, and even the ringing doorbell. Yes, I am embarrassed to admit it, but I would hide until whoever was at the door left. I apologize now if that was you I shunned. I could not face anyone. My face had not received the message that this was a family matter that needed to be neatly covered. I was grieving. As I grieved, it seemed as if a sense of hopelessness rushed in and engulfed me. I had become encapsulated. Every ounce of hope I had held onto for my son's entire life withdrew that evening, melting into a backdrop of nothingness. My world stopped. It was as if I was standing still and a massive F5 tornado was swirling all around me. I could not see anything. I could barely hear anything. Sounds intense and dramatic, I know. I lived it. I rarely do anything half-heartedly, including grieving evidently – but, I am here today to speak into someone's heart, into someone's darkness, that you can survive, and even thrive again! All hope is not lost, even when circumstances do not turn out the way we would like for them to. You can do the hard things in life! God will help you if you allow Him to. As I began to process the situation and enter into the different stages of my grief, I was able to hold onto impossible hope because of my relationship with my Heavenly Father. I chose to sit with Jesus in my ugly.

That November night my world stopped. At some point, I realized the house full of friends we had over for small group had dismissed themselves. I should have felt terrible about it all, even embarrassed, but the truth is I did not. I wanted to be alone. Eli's entire life had been spotted like a leper with behavioral and mental health issues; the culmination reaching a pinnacle that evening where we knew action had to ensue. It must. This time there was a victim, and my heart broke. I could not rescue my son – I did not need to rescue my son. My heart ached in ways I did not know was possible, for both the victim and my child. The complexity of the emotions I experienced was too difficult for me to give words to. How could I give birth to someone who could have done such a thing? This entire season would open the doors to a new season in life where I would learn to love my son from a distance while entrusting him completely to God.

Even during the storm, I still knew my child needed me more now than he had ever needed me before. Isn't this a beautiful picture of God sending His son to earth on a rescue mission! In the ugliness of sin, God knew we needed Him more than ever! Friend, whatever you are concealing in your life is suffocating you. Whatever "it" is that has stolen your breath, release it to God and allow Him to breathe fresh air into your lungs. There is nothing that will zap vitality out of you quicker than suppressing pain. It doesn't have to be packaged up in a pretty Christianity box with a nice, neat bow. God isn't scared of our ugly. He just wants us. For a while, I could not understand the part about not fearing, but now I clearly see. I was fearful of what others would think if they knew. I was afraid if people knew what my son did it would reflect our family and thus destroy the non-profit we headed up. God finally got through my thick skull that I am not my son's choices. My adult son chose to do what he did, not me. Even though I was suffering because of his choices, they did not define me as a person. God has not given us a spirit of fear. He desires for us to live in freedom, and in power, and to possess a sound mind. He desires for us to glean strength from Him and the power of His might to overcome tragedies in our lives here on earth. We are not promised a pain-free life. We are promised that we will not walk alone in those moments if we dare to trust and believe. It is moments and seasons like these that develop and stretch us as we are growing from Glory to Glory.

Eli is a brilliant, smart, and witty young man. He can be funny and entertaining, clever and sharp, and not afraid to march to the beat of his very own drum. He can understand and separate right from wrong. He is extremely high functioning. Eli has always been capable of making good, healthy, life-giving, and sustaining choices. Although more difficult for him, choosing to do what was right was not impossible. It was a matter of Eli's personal will and desire. Unfortunately, he often chose whichever path was easiest and required the least of him. He struggles to this day with appropriate boundaries and social interactions. He tends to become violent when triggered past his ability to cope with certain stimuli. He has a natural bent towards manipulation and instant self-gratification, with an inefficient radar or gauge of how his actions are impacting others. This has been hard to temper with the reality that he could understand right from wrong. He regularly stumped his psychiatrist and psychologist, leaving them scratching their heads in search of answers. If being honest, at times he did not seem to care, just as long as he got what he wanted in the moment. There were complete segments of his childhood and adolescence where he showed no remorse, yet other times where he could be a compassionate and gentle teddy bear. Often Eli struggled with authority issues, mainly with those of the opposite sex. He generally was submissive to same-sex authority figures, although not always. Eli also had moments of paranoia and hallucinations. On one occasion he described seeing shadows in his room telling him to, *"do it."* When asked what he thought that meant he would shrug his shoulders saying, *"I think they want me to hurt you."* More often than not, Eli chose instant gratification over hard work to be successful in areas he wanted to pursue and know more about. If something was hard, he would not give any effort. He often checked out anytime accountability and responsibility were required. This made it increasingly difficult as he got older to cultivate gifts and talents in his life. He refused to follow rules and would choose to incorrectly take advantage of coping skills, reverting to them as escape mechanisms instead.

    I have suffered abuse at the hand of my son - physical, mental, and emotional. I have been pinned to the wall, hit, bitten, cursed, clawed, and had my hair pulled out. I have had hot and cold liquids poured over me while being pushed down and held against the wall against my will (by a child that was 100 pounds larger than me), all to prove he had the upper hand - that he was in control and not me. I have had furniture hurled at my head and Christmas trees thrown across the living room. I have lived a nightmare with him. A nightmare in which no one would believe the truth, because something so dramatic could not possibly be true. I have managed to keep our car from going off the road multiple times as he would attack me while driving; often screaming as if he were possessed by a demon. I have had our home destroyed through his fits of rage and violence where the destruction was so severe, I wasn't initially allowed by the police to re-enter the home. I have slept with a deadbolt lock on my bedroom door in fear for my life. I have hidden kitchen knives and scissors in my closet instead of the kitchen drawers where they belonged. I have lived in a continual space of always looking over the shoulder to see what was coming next, never able to rest. I have listened to well-meaning individuals try to encourage me by telling me this was just a stage he was going through and he would eventually grow out of it if I just trusted God.

Eli's universal view and reality being parallel to that of actual reality makes this even more difficult. The combined impact of love and anger one feels is immeasurable on the parenting charts. I had spent his entire life grasping at every straw in hopes it would provide the answer, yet the answers never came. Life simply became exhausting, leaving me completely exasperated, and traumatized by the time he was 16 years old. The level of hopelessness I felt left me speechless. With very little assistance, I searched to no avail for self-help books for parents raising abusive and mentally ill children. I have had the state tell me it wasn't their job to raise my son, when all I was seeking was preventative care instead of reactive and punitive punishment. I remember screaming at God one afternoon, pleading with Him to please take one of us out of our misery. This is raw honesty guys. God is not looking for pretty. He is looking for real. He is not scared of our ugly. That afternoon as I cried for God to please make things easier, He gently answered me with, *"Make it easier for who?"*

I do not believe the human heart is designed to feel the weight of such an enormous throb as I was experiencing. Chances are, many of you reading this have experienced your own nightmare that you long to have freedom over. Only Jesus can carry the nightmare weight of your life. He desperately longs to carry all that is crushing us, but it is our choice to allow Him to carry the load. Allowing Jesus to carry my load did not automatically create a seismic explosion that vibrated my core and changed the landscape of my life. Nothing miraculous in the natural realm changed in the moment I chose complete surrender. Thinking back, my heart was in spasms for months and months, the latest news being the straw that broke the camel's back so to speak. It was the culmination of years of abuse, striving, trauma, and failure after failure colliding with this final straw. Yet, I chose to remain with a fixed focus because shifting my focus for even a second would leave me proclaiming what a cruel joke on humanity all this was. Shifting my focus for one moment would cause me to go off course and fall back into destructive patterns. I had a choice. I did not choose this reality, but I could choose my response. I could choose to go through the door leading to life instead of death. This was the moment of no return. I was standing on the banks of the river crossing and I had to choose to either cross over or turn back in retreat. Either way, nothing would ever be the same. Either I was going to choose to trust God in my deep pain, or not.

This moment was not a once-and-done type of moment for me, but rather a process. A long and difficult process. An ugly and continual process. I cried out daily. Sometimes every hour of every day. I screamed and shook my fist at the ceiling. I remember screaming to God one day, *"When is enough going to be enough?"* Life was ugly, and I was tired.

Did you know our ugly doesn't scare, offend, or anger God?

Someone needs to hear that. Read it again! He invites us to bring our ugly to Him. He wants our ugly. We do not have to clean it up and dress it up before bringing it to Him. We come just as we are and lay it all down at the foot of the Cross. It is only through the Cross that we find the ability to rise and overcome. It is only through the Cross we are made capable of love. It is only through the Cross we are given the ability to forgive. It is only through the

Cross of Christ that we find strength for the journey of a million miles. We will find this is the place endurance meets up with perseverance and determination.

Every year we love taking water-rafting trips to the Nantahala Outdoor Center. I will admit, I was a little apprehensive at first, but nonetheless, excited! Rafting had long been a bucket-list item for me for many years. My husband had rafted once before on the iconic and notably more dangerous and adventurous Ocoee River. To ease me into this thrill-seeking desire of my courageous, lionhearted, and fearless heart, he booked us a tour-guided rafting trip. Our excursion began in Bryson City as we made our way to our destination via the Old Smoky Mountain Railroad. We had seats in one of the open cars and a boxed lunch had been provided. Winding through, the views of Fontana Lake, Appalachian Trails, and track-side ferns and mountain laurels were charming and breathtaking. My heart was overwhelmed with gratitude that God would allow this little country girl to experience something so amazingly wonderful. I never could have believed growing up that I would ever be able to experience such thrill and beauty, much less travel to places I'd never known of or heard of. Fast forward, I now feel like a professional water-rafting queen since I have been down the Nantahala's Class II and Class III frigid rapids four times, and have lived to boast of my survival.

We recently took our annual trip to Nantahala with friends who volunteer with the non-profit we run. Every time, no matter how many times you run these rapids and despite how much you think you might know, protocol requires you to sit through a video and safety tutorial presentation. This time our instructor gave some instructions I had not previously heard, or even considered. Natural human tendency is to look at the obstacles in front of us. In this case, the obstacles were the rocks, boulders, or trees in the water. The ultimate goal, of course, is for your raft not to become lodged or stuck on one of these obstructions. Should that happen – well, most likely you would flip out of your boat and land in the water. When you are looking directly at the rock you are trying to avoid, despite how fast and hard you are trying to paddle the raft in another direction, you naturally gravitate more toward the very thing you are looking at. This forces you to work harder and harder to try and avoid it, exhausting you and your entire crew. I can still hear our instructor saying, *"Look away, look at where you are wanting to go instead of what is in front of you."* How often do we give our sustained focus to the difficulties and drawbacks of life, analyzing and trying to figure out how to best overcome or avoid the obstructions altogether, instead of focusing on where we are wanting to go? How many times do we get stuck because all we can see is the problem? How many times have we missed the mark because we can't take our eyes off everything that is wrong? How many times do we become paralyzed in fear? How many times do we get trapped in prolonged cycles of desperation, exhausting ourselves in arduous attempts to keep our heads above the waters we are treading? When we are more focused on what is hindering our progress than the advantage of keeping our eyes focused - it is then that our hope, our purpose, and our destiny get off course and begin to gravitate in the opposite direction we need to be headed.

In our case, we ended up stuck on top of a very large rock for what seemed like an eternity. Despite our attempts to avoid becoming stuck, we forgot the instructions given and found it hard not to focus on the boulder we had been trying to avoid. The waters were fierce and picked us up and plopped us down right on top of it as if we were its trophy. We had six people in our boat. We shifted our weight from one end of the raft to the other. It was a rather comical sight in retrospect. Where are the video cameras when you need them? I am certain this video would have won the grand prize on America's Funniest Home Videos! The force of the water and rapids had us convinced of the inevitable upturning, in which we would all be left fending for our lives as we floated down the freezing Nantahala. At one point our raft was almost perpendicular and shifting from left to right, as if in a vertical position of waving farewell, while we were all on top of one another and unable to move. Strangely enough, I could not stop laughing. Such an odd way to kiss the safety of the raft goodbye in this most impressive and outstanding display of rafting expertise. We rocked frontwards and backwards and sideways, using our oars to try and dislodge our raft. Other rafters and kayakers passing by offered assistance and advice. Much to our dismay, we remained stuck, despite our efforts and their assistance. Eventually, we were able to dislodge our previously immovable raft and continue our voyage down the river with shouts and cheers of joy!

Thinking back to this season of life when our world stopped at the news of our son, I did not withdraw from God as I had done so many times previously in my life. I did not keep my focus on the pain and shock of the situation. Although initially frozen in the gravity of the news, I entered the reality of the pain instead of ignoring it. I forced myself to look at where I wanted to go instead of where I was. I forced myself to keep my focus fixed on the hope God had called me into. I did not do it perfectly. It was not easy and breezy by any stretch of the imagination. However, I decided to not trust my feelings and human instincts, despite the magnetic field surrounding me, trying to repel truth and love.

Every magnet has two sides: a south pole and a north pole. When you align two magnets with the south pole of one facing the north pole of the other, they will be drawn to one another. This is where we get our saying, "opposites attract." Not only are the two magnets drawn to one another, they are forced to stick to one another. Their power will also draw other magnets. However, magnets will not always be drawn to one another. Growing up I recall being mesmerized by this magnetic push and pull phenomenon; this dance of attract and repel. If you hold the magnets where the same poles are next to one another, the magnetic field surrounding them will push away and they will resist one another. Interesting. It is only when you are holding the opposite poles next to one another that they attract and are drawn to one another.

Have you ever heard the statement, "misery loves company?" The sentiment is that sometimes when we are suffering and in pain, we oddly find comfort in being surrounded by more misery and pain. Although I had never wanted others to suffer in the same way I had been afflicted, I found a peculiar security and contentment of sorts in the familiarity of my pain. When my misery met with more of the same (two like poles aligned), it would repel and push away the very thing I needed to attract. The darker my distress, and the deeper my pain, the further away I would push true comfort and serenity found in the peace of God. I would push away the love and affection of others, and the connection found in community. Satan knows we are stronger together and for this reason, he aims to isolate us. When I was finally able to flip the magnetic poles to where my misery was now aligned with truth (opposite poles), I found myself deeply attracted to the only thing that could heal my brokenness – Jesus! I found myself stuck to the immovable and unchangeable word of truth. I found myself penetrated to the core by hope. I was bonded to the unshakeable, unmistakable, and undeniable presence of God. His mighty hand was irrefutable, His involvement most definitely undisputable, His accuracy was incontestable, His amazingly beautiful compassion was unwavering, and His promises were irrevocable in my life. And – they still are!

I chose to trust what I knew to be true, even when I could not see it or feel it. The prayer I prayed went something like this:

God, I recognize that I don't know much, so I won't waste my time praying about things I don't know much about. I choose to not focus and dwell on the hurt, the pain, and the inability to understand someone else and their motives. I choose to stop placing a magnifying glass over the problems I cannot solve. I will not pretend to try and understand a broken world. Instead, I will pray about things I know something of. I know that You are good. I know that You are God. I know You are good to me. I know You are good for me. I do not know what else to pray. So, help me through the Cross, because I cannot do this without You. I choose to focus on where I want to go instead of where I am.

I only knew this simple truth because I had become intimate with truth through an intentional effort to forge a relationship with God; a relationship forged on the anvil of pain and surrender. I chose to hide His truth in my heart for such times as this. I sat at the foot of the Cross with my broken heart, sobbing. I had to fight to retain the few good memories I had with my son. Despite my every effort to hold on to them, they seemed to slowly be slipping away. This is not something you rush to sign up for. This is not a notable club to be a member of; yet I have learned it is bursting at the seams with fellow comrades. Satan fought hard to keep me silent, cloaked in shame under the guile, deceitful tactics, and lies that shouted I was the only one. He still fights hard to this day to silence me. There were many times I believed his lies too. I believed that no one else would ever believe my story, or desire to be associated with me if they knew my ugly. For this reason, my next book will be a memoir of loving my son and our journey through the dimensions of God's extraordinary love and grace. Our greatest battle moments are when we realize we are not alone, never have been alone, and never will be alone. Our greatest battle moments are when we finally realize that it is not by our strength, might, and power, but by God's! God within us and for us is all we need! He is a good God! He is so good! This truth makes us the majority, and not the minority.

CHAPTER 8
FORGIVE and FORGET
But – Did God Really Say That?

There's an age-old adage I've heard most of my life - *"forgive and forget."* This *"let bygones be bygones"* anthem rambled through my head and was embedded into every fiber of my being, echoing through much of my life. I think it mostly brings comfort to the offender by providing a rapid cliche escape from the discomfort of sitting with the truth of their actions; thus, placing the entire weight upon the shoulders of whoever was on the other end of their deeds.

For me, I truly believed if I could not forget something, then I had not truly forgiven and was a terrible person. If I could not forgive, then God would not forgive me. If I could not be forgiven by God, then what was the point because there would be no hope for me. *(Stick with me. I will bring clarity to the above statements shortly.)* My belief in this way of thinking presented a terrible obstruction to the truth being able to freely flow into my heart. The problem with an adage is it should by its very definition express a general truth. This maxim and rule of conduct demanded I follow the guidelines of etiquette set in place by society, and even by well-meaning - yet gravely misinformed - Christians. The proverbial truth that *"time heals all wounds"* danced around in my head like raindrops falling from the sky, splattering, and then being absorbed into the ground beneath it. Those drops of rain are what life felt like - like a treacherous rainstorm that left me broken, spilled out, and absorbed into the sequential cadences of life. One after another, my heartaches went marching down this path - like little ants marching one by one. This socially driven pattern of behavior mandated I align myself with a belief system that preached:

FORGIVENESS = PARDON
FORGIVENESS = ABSOLUTION

The problem with an adage is that it contains just enough truth to sound, for the most part, reasonable and believable. Its credibility is founded in the probable theory presented – the theory that the outcome of humanity hinges on my ability instead of God ability. I believed, through the conditioning of my heart, that if I could not find a way to wipe my memory like a clean slate of all that had and has happened, then perhaps I had not truly forgiven and therefore I could not be forgiven. If I could never be forgiven, then what would be the point of even trying? The lie played like a broken record in my mind. If I could not flip the switch like the light switch on the wall, then I was still walking in unforgiveness. This was an impassible mountain to scale.

Y'all, nothing could be further from the actual truth than this right here. This sham has conned many of their peace and crippled them from ever finding lasting freedom. Nowhere in the Holy Bible does it declare we must forgive and adapt spiritual amnesia to be redeemed by our Father. A "Holy forgetting" of pain and trauma that God gifts His children with through the processes of deep spiritual and emotional healing is so very often misinterpreted and misrepresented. God can and will remove certain memories from us, but forgetting our past will never build a healthy future. Deceptions and half-truths such as this worn-out adage breed insecurity. Insecurity will keep us in a perpetuating endless cycle of doubt, unbelief, and hesitation; always second-guessing ourselves and others. Hesitation will give way to impairment of our sight as it obstructs our vision, dictating what we can and cannot see. Satan is tricky. He knows the right combination of truth mixed with a lie that will cause humanity to pause and question, like in the Garden of Eden…

Did God Really Say?

I struggled greatly with the whole *"forgiving and forgetting"* platitude because I have been forgiven so much - and, because of that forgiveness I am incredibly grateful that my Abba sees the atonement instead of my sin. The Cross washes our many sins as far as the east is from the west in a moment of true repentance and surrender, never to be remembered again. That is a key point to take note of because this is where Satan can mix a little truth with a big lie and muddle the certainty we have in and through Christ Jesus.

It is conceivable to see how a skewed definition of forgiveness gets twisted and leads to an inability to see the atonement that has been made. It is easy to see how this interpretation leaves a person aching and longing their entire life; leaving them paralyzed and rendering them ineffective. It plants seeds of doubt as one begins to believe they will never be able to measure up to God's standards, much less to the flawed and broken standard of man and culture. But friends, hear me when I say this - forgiveness and healing are not synonymous. Not even close. **Forgiveness is a choice. Healing is a process. And just perhaps, it may be that remembrance is a gift.**

I suppose you could say my life has closely resembled a game of Twister with all the bending over backwards like a warped Gumby figure. Exasperating efforts have gone into trying to hold myself together, into following all the rules, and giving my best to remain strong and steady. Just like in the game, however, I would come crashing down somewhere along the way. The wrists become shaky. The knees become wobbly. Then – BAM! You're out! This adage of *"forgive and forget"* is much like a game of Twister. It is nearly impossible to twist and bend with all the game demands and keep it all together. It is not a matter of **IF** we will come crashing down, but rather, **WHEN**!

How do you forget all the pain? How do you forget the damage caused? The impact? How do you live every single day of your life as if nothing ever happened? How do you do that? How do you simply flip the switch and move forward, skipping along the proverbial yellow brick road to happiness? How do you forget the abuse? How do you forget the disrespect? How do you forget the years lost in chaos, confusion, and pain? How do you forget that feeling of being disposable? How do you forget the place of loneliness and isolation caused by the choices and dysfunctions of others? How do you simply flip a switch and say, *"Oh, you're sorry? Okay, I'm good now. Thank you."* I am with you, friends. Forgiveness at times can seem an outrage against justice and humanity. Stick with me here. These are all questions I have asked myself. I am very well acquainted with these perplexing feelings and emotions. I too have struggled to temper this line of thinking and reasoning with what the Bible charges us with. There have been moments I would have rather poked my eyeballs out than sit with the uncomfortableness of facing this part of my life. When we ask God to search us, to know us, and to show us things we need to address (Psalm 139: 23-24) – buckle up because He is faithful to do so.

How do you marry love and forgiveness with pain and sin? This is the million-dollar question. We start with choosing to focus our attention on the truth of Scripture and by choosing to change our thought patterns. Satan prides himself on confusing God's standards with mankind's ideals and canons for living! I had never once stopped to consider the overwhelming truth that God CHOSE to forgive me and remember my sins no more. The atonement represents the healing balm. The Bible does not say God cannot remember; He chooses not to remember. He chooses to see the value in me, His child. Likewise, we have been given opportunity as well to see the value in others. In my repentance, God chooses to see the Blood of Jesus, the redemptive and healing atonement paid to wash my sins clean. My sin is no longer held against me. No longer is God's heart broken over my actions, rather it is rejoicing in my choice of complete surrender. There is a big difference. God can do all things, so surely, He can remember as well. He simply chooses not to. He chooses the healing balm. He is God, and I - well, I am not God. This revelation is a beautiful picture of the perfect love of God that possesses the ability to cast out all my fears if I will allow it to!

Don't you love Magic Erasers? They have to be the best creation since Oreo cookies in my opinion. *(That is, back when I still ate Oreo cookies – that's for another book.)* Magic Erasers are relatively little, yet incredibly mighty. They can remove crayons from painted walls, soap scum rims from the bathtub, and skid marks from my favorite white tennis shoes without much effort on my end. I'm not exactly sure what's in one of those little magic rectangles, but whatever it is – I'm in love with it. When truth invades and takes over, we begin to understand that forgiveness is not like one of these glorious Magic Erasers.

Most often we are shocked to discover when we extend forgiveness to someone who has wronged us, we are the ones who experience liberation. The offense against us no longer has the power to continue hurting us over and over. Forgiveness is not freedom from the responsibility of action for the perpetrator. It is relinquishing my right to punish the one who hurt me as I release all power to God and His justice system. As I choose forgiveness and start the healing journey, God begins to soften my aching heart. I sense a calming that whispers to my soul – *let go*! Whatever God decides to do is best because He is in control and has a bird's eye view I do not. I begin to embrace God as my defender. Forgiveness recognizes my inability to forgive and love except through the power of the Cross. Jesus forgave me of my sins and washed me as white as snow because of the Cross. This does not magically erase the fact that I was guilty. It does mean, however, that sin and guilt no longer have the power to control my destiny. The Blood of Jesus and His forgiveness restores me to the opportunity to live in freedom. Forgiveness does not always mean reconciliation with someone who harmed me or that I harmed, although it can be a component. Forgiveness never requires me to pretend or live in denial either. Forgiveness only requires the actions of one person – me! Forgiveness is an exertion of steps I take that will release not only the offender but me as well! My actions will open the door to the healing of trauma while also opening the door for God to work in and through the situation. It is my choice though. I get to decide. So do you, my friend.

Let us be clear about something. Forgiveness is not the same as healing. The choice to forgive is singular. The choice to enter the healing process is multi-dimensional. This is an extremely important distinction to recognize. This is where the enemy mixes untruth with truth so he can deposit confusion into the hearts and minds of people. By nature, healing usually requires time and processes. Because of this, we cannot expect to ignore the healing element in search of our recovery. This is also a case and point of why an inability to forget does not mean we have not chosen to walk in forgiveness. It is easy to lump forgiveness and healing into the same category. Not intentionally, but somewhere on a subconscious level it naturally happens to many of us. While we know in our minds that they are not the same, we live our lives every day as if they are. Our hearts have not received the message and truth that our brains already know about. We sincerely pray and ask God to forgive us, and He is faithful to do so. We forgive others for how they have wronged us and we choose to walk daily in that forgiveness. We know that forgiveness is a choice and our feelings and emotions will eventually follow suit. We ask for the forgiveness of others when needed and pray they extend it back to us. We pray the prayers that break the bondages, strongholds, and curses off our lives, and yet we somehow miss and overlook the red flag warnings that we were wounded and in need of healing. We are masters at placing Band-Aids on gunshot wounds and expecting the miraculous to happen. The event(s) that caused trauma are in the past, forgiven, under the Blood, and we have moved on like good little Christians. Yet, this truth remains - the trauma caused by the impact of that period in our lives lingers. We become stuck. Sometimes we are years down the road before we realize we are trapped and in need of a rescue mission.

My husband and I walked through a very dark season when we first got married. The first three and a half years were nothing short of miserable for both of us, as well as for our children, friends, and family who all had front-row seats to our three-ring circus. Tom held fast to his self-protective mechanisms and

I would become despondent in my longing for the story-book romance. Those years were much like the free-fall drop Tower of Terror ride at Six Flags. You know, the one that slowly raises you up, then out of nowhere drops you, only to raise you back up and drop you again? You've barely had time to catch your breath before the next drop. You are being jerked back and forth so quickly that you feel like a rubber band about to break. That is what our life was like. The thing about brokenness is that it not only affects us, but it impacts all of those we care for and love the most as well. Brokenness causes a person to become blind to the impact of the storm on those around them.

Tom and I both were assuming, accusing, and condemning of one another. These behavior patterns played out in every other area of our marriage as well. We both had unresolved relationship and family issues from our past that we carried as baggage into our new marriage. Neither one of us was willing to help the other unpack that baggage once and for all. Partly because we kept much of our hurt tucked beneath the surface in fear of being hurt again. We did not feel it was safe to share too much or too deeply. For me, my vulnerability in the past had already been used as a weapon against me, and I was not about to allow that to happen again. We had a self-seeking marriage with a contract mentality where the fear of "divorce" was always lurking and used as a weapon to walk the tightrope.

Tom and I both had unrealistic expectations of one another. We held each other to impossible standards with measures that could never be reached. We looked to each other to fill needs that only God could meet. We did not prioritize our marriage or one another. Our main goal was to protect ourselves, despite any love we felt for one another. We consistently chose to rank the health of our marriage as second to external influences in their many forms. And, there were many – but that is for another book. Let me encourage you right now – if there is a voice that is being given a space in your marriage outside of God and your spouse, you need to cut that voice off immediately! Sever it. God is first, and your marriage and spouse are second. That is God's design and the order of priority. You must decide what matters most to you. You cannot allow fear and external influences to impact the health and wellness of your unity. If you do, your marriage will not survive, and that my friend is the goal of our enemy. Every single time an external voice is allowed to take a front row seat in your marriage, your spouse will be moved to the backseat and left feeling like a third wheel. It communicates to them that they do not matter to you.

Traditional families are not without their struggles and they certainly take much work to be successful. Blended families, however, are never easy and breezy - even on their best days. It takes a lot of giving, flexing, patience, forgiveness, and compromise from all sides. ALL SIDES. Inevitably, without a carefully sustained and intentional focus, the marriage begins to slide down a slippery slope into a pit of muck. Do you know what muck is? It is waste matter. It's garbage - a pit of dirt and grime, mess and ickiness. Can you imagine? What a visual! Yuck! If we could peek into the spiritual realm and see what is really going on, we would see the sewer of our lives where Satan has held us captive in all our disillusionments; in the muck. Our marriage began on a faulty foundation and therefore never had a chance of surviving the impact of those first few years of testing. Neither one of us had experienced the healing of past wounds and continued to wound one another. Neither one of us understood the dynamics and dimensions of what a healthy marriage relationship looked like. Band-Aids were placed on our gaping gunshot wounds and we would continue marching on until we were wounded again. Much like wounded animals, we were easy and vulnerable prey. When an animal is wounded it will become desperately defensive, even aggressive, in an instinctive attempt to protect itself from further injury or attacks. This phenomenon is not something we only see in animals though. This behavior is prominent in humans as well. When

Tom and I would perceive a threat or attack coming close, our fangs and nails came out in defense. I ultimately was left feeling incredibly vulnerable and insecure.

Addictions were rampant. We lived a double life. We attended church and even served on the Dream Team. I am about to lay many of our cards on the table for you. You need to see how bad the situation was, and how deep the lies ran. We were small group leaders, even co-leading a Freedom group; ignoring the fact we were both in desperate need of healing and freedom ourselves. We played the game well. We were imposters though. We were the greatest pretenders on the face of the earth – and we maintained this posture for a season. We fooled many – that is, until we could no longer fool them, or even ourselves. I remember after one Freedom Conference, we jumped into the car to head towards the hotel. As I was driving, Tom grabbed a beer from the cooler in the backseat. *(Let us not forget we were leaving a Freedom Conference at our church, guys – a conference in which we were serving.)* We were only a short 10-minute drive from the hotel, yet the addiction was so strong, he could not wait. The pattern continued throughout the evening. Several hurtful incidences occurred that night, bleeding over into the next morning. We both woke up feeling hung over and detached. Tom had a weakness for alcohol abuse and had grown up with an alcoholic father. *(He has made peace with his father and offered and received forgiveness.)* Tom drank to numb the intense pain he felt on the inside, as well as to avoid conflict resolution. He despised conflict because he had never seen healthy forms of conflict modeled when he was growing up. He struggled to see how conflict in any form could ever be constructive and beneficial. I did not struggle as intensely with alcoholism as Tom did, meaning I could have taken it or left it. I should have left it! Although I had a much higher tolerance level, I drank equally as much to deal with his drinking, to numb my pain, and to hopefully avoid upsetting him in any way. I would numb my soul so I would not object to or reject whatever the night would throw my way. Read that last sentence again. That is not the marker of a healthy relationship. My heart's sole desire was to make Tommy happy. That is the problem though. Humans were never meant to be each other's little "g" gods. Only God himself can give an individual true healing, resolution, and redeem all the hurt in their lives. Only God can be someone's everything. The morning dawned with a new upset that left him angry, and left me gravely misunderstood and distraught. Tom and I got ourselves dressed, gave each other the silent treatment and cold shoulder, and headed back to the church to assume our roles during the remainder of the Freedom Conference. Several times that day I started to call my mom to come and pick me up, and yet I stayed because I could not bear the thought of upsetting Tom and losing him forever. The next several weeks would be overshadowed by a dark cloud of hurt and many instances of the wounded-animal phenomenon.

Tom and I carried brokenness into our marriage and begin to construct a life on a foundation that was never going to be able to support the weight of our infrastructure. Our cynicism and sarcasm bred more of the same. We did not have trust. We were suspicious of one another without cause. We set each other up for failure and then pointed our fingers at one another when we would fall. We created our own storm and then screamed in unbelief when the storm overwhelmed us. We were disrespectful and hateful with our speech - all as forms of protective mechanisms for our badly wounded and broken hearts. We did not love, honor, respect, or serve one another. We served the god of self instead of doing our best to meet each other's needs in the context of a healthy and God-centered marriage. We often accused one another even when there was nothing to be accused of. Of course, this would lead to hurt feelings and ultimately a refusal to put forth more effort; the cycle was perpetuating. If you are constantly looking for the bad, you will find it. If you are constantly expecting your spouse to fail you, I promise you they will. If you are consistently looking for a reason to prove your rightness and their wrongness, you will find it. If you only see the bad and never the good, you will never have a beautiful life. Not ever. If you always expect perfection, you will always be disappointed.

Depression began to grip our minds and hearts. Tom and I allowed deception from the enemy to sneak into our home and it nearly brought us completely down – I'm talking six feet under. The enemy of our souls could see purpose and destiny written all over our lives even though we could not see it at the time. Because of this, he was seeking to destroy us before we ever recognized what was going on. The opinion of someone outside of our marriage was consistently allowed to sow fear and uncertainty into our marriage with their threats and attempts to wreak havoc in our lives. I believe this was because of a past injury that had not been healed in their life.

In 2018, Tom called me from Japan and told me to be gone by the time he returned home. He made some threats to guarantee my compliance. He cut me off financially for the second time. This would ultimately lead to the second time he would serve me divorce papers within a 2 ½ year period of time. This marked twice I had now packed my belongings and like a dog with my tail tucked between my legs had moved out. That is the only way I know how to describe it. I was heartbroken and angry at the same time. The feelings of being completely disposable, embarrassed, invisible, defeated, unattractive, defective, and lonely were overwhelming. Because I had been cut off financially and didn't have access to our accounts, I felt a complete sense of hopelessness to do anything about my situation.

A few months prior to this culmination of events, the darkness and hollowness had become so piercing that I tried to take my life twice with a cocktail of over-the-counter drugs, prescription drugs, and alcohol. Each time I would wake up to find my attempts unsuccessful and my heart would sink that I had to endure another day. No one in my life knew how bad off I was. I hid it well to insure and protect my control, as well as to underwrite my intentions. I could not have anyone attempting to thwart my plans. By July of the same year, separated again and facing divorce yet again, Tom found himself suicidal and severely depressed as well.

Broken people break people guys. Hurting people hurt people. It doesn't make them bad people. It makes them wounded people. This breaks the heart of God. People who know Tommy and I today find it hard to believe when we share intimate details of our story. They cannot comprehend how callous we used to be. If we do not understand why we are the way we are, then we will never be able to overcome it. This is why simply forgetting our past is not helpful in the healing process. If we simply desire to erase and forget the past because it hurts, then we can never process through it, grow from it, learn from it, and become better. We cannot have a future if we try to obliterate the past. Adapting spiritual amnesia is not the same as healing. That is called denial. Only God can heal and redeem the past. Only God can convert brokenness into something beautiful. Only God can take the ashes of a life and declare destiny and purpose. The Word of God, the truth of God tells us that we are overcomers not only by the Blood shed at Calvary, but also by the word of our testimonies. Satan seeks to silence us so we never discover that we are not alone in our journey and struggles. This is why he uses that adage we mentioned at the beginning of this chapter to confuse and distort God's children. We need one another and the strength found in the context of community and connection. Satan almost succeeded in placing yet another generational curse of suicide upon our lineage through the open doors that gave him legal access. It was only in recognizing this, in doing all the hard work to overcome and close those doors, that we are who we are today and where we are today. We had to address the past to move forward. We could not simply forgive and forget the past. When I think about all God has blessed us with through the work we do with our non-profit, and how it almost never was, I cannot help but fall at the foot of the Cross in continued surrender and gratitude.

Sometimes we stay in our pain because it's familiar. Strangely, in that familiarity we find comfort. To change and heal takes hard work. It takes courage. It takes heart. Scripture tells us in *John 8:32, "WE SHALL KNOW THE TRUTH, AND THE TRUTH SHALL SET US FREE."* We must allow truth to saturate us to the core, despite how much it may hurt. Simply being acquainted with the truth is not enough. Having knowledge of God is not the same as being in relationship with God. We must take hold of the power of what the truth is, not the power of what we believe the truth to be. Freedom is found in the KNOWING and the application of what is known! This exposure to the very heart of our God opens an entirely new dimension of freedom that we were created to encounter and enjoy. Knowing and applying the truth that forgiveness is a choice found in surrender and repentance, and that healing is not dependent upon my ability to "snap out of it" and get with the program is refreshing; it brings hope - it gives birth to joy.

We do not have to live very long before experiencing being hurt or offended by someone else. Hurt has varying degrees and can be caused by a loved one, or someone we do not know at all. Unforgiveness by design keeps us imprisoned and forever connected to our offender in an unhealthy way. This connection in turn wreaks havoc in our lives. It is possible to forgive without forgetting. Sometimes we do not need to forget. Forgetting means we lose the lessons learned. We often cannot build healthy futures if we destroy the past and pretend it never happened. If we do not remember where we come from, how will we ever know where we are going? How do we give thanks to God for something we cannot recall? How can we become overcomers by both the Blood of the Lamb and the word of our testimonies if we cannot recall our past? I believe you can effectively walk in forgiveness and complete healing, without forgetting. I believe you can come to a place of healing that allows you to walk into a place of forgiveness that does not house the sting of pain anymore. I would not be sitting here today typing out this memoir of my life if I begged God to remove it from my memory. Think about that for a moment. Or, how about this? If Christ wanted the pain of the Cross wiped from His memory, how would He ever remember the atonement made and see that instead of our sin?

 I had a little chat with God one morning and decided I could be and would be brave. If my life story could somehow be a survival guide of sorts, pointing others to Jesus, then I could be brave, bold, and courageous. I could put myself on the line. I could do that. Remembering can be healthy and beneficial. Our remembering can be God's hands extended to someone else who is hurting. Forgiveness requires that I place my broken heart into the hands of Jesus and allow Him to mend it and choose how to use it. Choosing to become better instead of bitter and livelier instead of lonelier can be a lifeline to someone else living in despondency. We are not robots with erased memories every morning; however, we must choose to not dwell in the pain. It is our choice. Our position must be this - when Satan tries to replant old seeds of hurt and pain, remind him that he is trespassing and does not have legal access to us and ours.

And we know that in all things God works for the good of those who love him, who have been called according to his purpose. Romans 8:28 NIV

When we walk through the valley of the shadow of death – we must not pitch our tents and camp out there. It is healthy to process what has happened. It is necessary. It is a critical step in our healing that cannot be skirted around. Like the children's song, GOING ON A BEAR HUNT – *we cannot go over it, we can't go around it, can't go under it, got to go through it!* We cannot come through something we refuse to enter into. The timestamp is different for everyone, but when the time comes, we must stand once again. We must walk through the valley – not decide to build and live there. We must choose to not view everything else in life through the lens of pain and suffering either, but rather through the lens of God's Holy Word!

Have you ever thought about how God's plans for us are not based on our abilities but are contingent upon our choices and decisions? Our lives are the sum total of the choices and decisions we make. Our lives are always moving in the direction of our beliefs, opinions, and choices. Negative thoughts and choices will result in a negative life. Seems ridiculous to me that an all-knowing and all-capable God would entrust something as fragile and life-altering to me, an inadequate human. Yet, this is how His great love is defined. He loves us so much, and it is in that great love that He allows us to freely choose the life He has designed specifically for us. If He forced our hands, then our devotion would be pre-fabricated at best. Love and devotion cannot be forced. It must be chosen. Our sole reliance and love for God is not something that can be assembled on-site. It is manufactured piece by piece through the ruts and trenches of our lives spent in a sincere and unforced desire for the Father. Purpose and destiny are born in the trenches of life. Wisdom is born in the trenches of life. Generational bondages and curses are identified and broken in the trenches of life. It is in this place we discover others along the way and help them continue in their journey to healing. We get to choose. Our relationship with our Father is not one honed out of a *"because I said so,"* mentality, rather it is refined and perfected through the course of a lifetime spent honoring and drawing close to God.

I have always had this deep desire to understand something and choose for myself. It is true that Father always knows best, but He also desires that we learn and grow through the experiences of life, recognizing our completely bankrupt status without Him. If He were to force our choices and love, most likely we would never learn that complete surrender and obedience to His ways are the best choice for our lives. As the Son of God was about to embrace and go through the greatest struggle and trial of His life on earth, fulfilling the sole purpose He came, He cried,

…Abba, Father, all things are possible for you. Remove this cup from me. Yet not what I will, but what you will. Mark 14:36 ESV

CHAPTER 9
CHOICES

I grew up in a very small town. The nearest movie theaters, skating rinks, shopping malls, mini-golf courses, and arenas of any sorts were at a minimum 35-40 minutes away. The local dance hall had been a thing of days gone by and seemed to disappear altogether with the generation or two before me. My friends and I always loved when mom would agree to take us to the roller-skating rink. For a small-town kiddo, the roller-skating rink was like "painting the town red." Kids these days will never understand the joy found in roller skating, especially backwards – an ability I never quite seemed to be well endowed with, but I could hold my own as long as no one bumped into me. It was almost like trying to roller-skate on ice honestly.

Once a month, twice if we were lucky, mom would drop us off for a few hours. What I did not know until years later was how she passed the time while we were having fun. She would cross the road to the Kmart Shopping Center. There she would sit for hours underneath the parking lot street light and read her book. In those days monthly shopping excursions were not within the budget, so curling up with a good book provided her mind time to relax and forget about much of the stress of life. She would patiently wait until it was time to pick us up. When I was 15 years old, I met a guy at the skating rink one night who was 19 years old. I knew my Mom and Dad would never approve of my dating this young man due to several painfully obvious reasons. First, he had already graduated from high school and I was a freshman. Secondly, I was not allowed to date until I was 16 years old, a rule that had been well-communicated in our home since I was old enough to know what a date was. This rule had been communicated so frequently that it played like a broken record inside my mind. Sixteen seemed like an eternity away to an anxious young girl however. We cooked up a plan that we would tell my Mom and Dad he was 18 years old. In our minds, 18 did not seem near as bad as 19 sounded. Hopefully, they would not ask about the whole school thing. Fingers crossed. There was one tiny little detail that we were both unaware of that jerked a knot in our rope instantly, outwitting our remarkably brilliant plan. You see, when I was a baby, our family lived right next door to this young man's family in the small town we lived in. Mom knew exactly who he was and she knew exactly how old was too! I was busted! My decision to choose unwisely and begin my dating years with a lie planted seeds of doubt in my parent's minds about whether I could be trusted without their physical presence.

Every single day we are faced with countless choices and decisions that need to be made. An article published in 2015 by Dr. Joel Hoomans at Roberts Wesleyan College sites that we make on average around 35,000 decisions every single day. The ability to choose and make our own decisions is a gift that has been entrusted to us; a gift we should each steward wisely. Each morning I must decide if I want to drink my coffee black, with the Chocolate Caramel Salt LMNT packet I love, or with added butter, ghee, or MCT oil – which I also LOVE! Yes, I am aware that this is a relatively trivial first-world frustration, but guys – it's real in my house! I must choose whether or not I will prioritize time in the word, worship, and in conversation, and listening to God. Every moment I am choosing where my focus will be given. Every moment I am choosing whether to be present or distracted. There is power to be found in a focused life. I get to choose every single day to put on the full armor of God that will equip me for whatever may be hurling toward me at lightning speed. I get to choose how I will dress, if I will exercise, what I will eat or not eat, and many other daily restorative, preservative, and protective details of life. Choosing to react in a moment, or practice the pause, giving the situation time to marinate within me, is a wisdom and discernment that only comes through a focused life. God empowers me to choose the path in which my thoughts will lead me; thoughts that ultimately dictate the trajectory of my day and entire life. The choices I make not only make me better, but they also make the world around me better. Think about that. Our courage today to make the right choices – the hard choices – the choices we may not feel like making - can impact entire generations to come. That is powerful guys. The choices we make are birthed out of our belief systems. Our belief systems are borne of our thought processes. Our thought processes are generated and wired from what we continuously allow our heart and mind to dwell upon; where our focus is. In Philippians 4:8, we are taught and encouraged to train our minds and hearts to think upon and dwell upon those things that are lovely, pure, honorable, commendable, praise-worthy, just, and true. Our daily choice to choose complete surrender and to follow God whole-heartily will never fail or disappoint us.

It is a daily decision to hope instead of despair. It is a daily and intentional effort to put one foot in front of the other instead of sitting and staring into nothingness. I'm not saying you are always going to feel like making the right choice, but this truth remains – we still have the privilege of choice. Our feelings will often lie to us. When we pre-determine that we will live a spirit-led life, even in the face of life's difficult moments, God will be there to help with the impossible parts. We do what we can and God does what only He can. It is a daily choice to surrender our schedules and busyness in exchange for an open hand, open heart, and open mind. It's a daily choice to choose kindness over callousness, love over hate, and generosity over selfishness. Every day we all have the choice to be flexible instead of demanding our own ways to manipulate outcomes. Daily we can choose the eternal over the here and now, joy despite the circumstances, peace instead of worry, and life instead of death. It is a daily choice to surrender my will to His will, my emotions to the leading of His Spirit, and my desires to His calling. It is a daily choice to lay aside pride that shouts intolerance and entitlement and to pick up the cross of selfless love and sacrifice. It is a daily choice to pre-decide that the course of my life will not be charted by fleeting emotional responses to temporal circumstances and situations. I can choose every single day to lean into the wisdom of choosing others over myself. Every day I have been given the opportunity to love others more than anything else my heart may be tempted to lean towards. It is a daily choice to shift my focus, change my lens, sharpen my view, and clear my vision.

Experiencing the blessing of God upon our lives requires the choice of completely surrendering our schedule to His interruptions. We do this by identifying the excess in our lives that is causing unnecessary stress. Identifying the non-essentials in our lives will not always guarantee a smooth ride, but it will allow space and margin when life or God interrupts our plans. I can assure you that the more determined you become about going hard and fast after your dream and purpose, the more distractions and busyness will seek to consume all your time and attention. I do mean ALL OF IT! And, plot twist - these distractions are not all bad. Some are even necessary and good. That is where we must implement healthy boundaries, exercise wisdom and discernment, become focused, and clear away any excess bidding for our time. In some seasons this may even mean hobbies and activities we enjoy must be placed on the shelf. Even as I am writing this morning, the timer is going off, the dryer just stopped, Grandpa John's clock my husband inherited is chiming every 15 minutes, my stomach is growling, and the phone will not stop dinging and ringing. Family and friends are calling, there are notifications, emails, and data entries for our non-profit that are begging for a piece of me, and discouragement is trying to wiggle its way into the mix through one of our adult children. My heart began racing until I remembered – I HAVE A CHOICE to be reactive or proactive. The beautiful gift God has given to each of us is the ability to choose which boundaries and rules to implement and adhere to in our lives. Each one of us has been given the same amount of time each day to accomplish our dreams and to take care of our responsibilities. Are we choosing wisely?

    Choosing wisely is something that no one else can do for us, not even God Himself. Our choices shape us. They shape our families. They shape our futures. The form our reputations. They shake foundations and change lives. The choices we make have a ripple effect that spreads into every connecting area of our lives. Our choices set us up for success or failure. They have huge implications on the lineage of our entire family line to come after us. Our decisions can take us down roads we never intended to destinations we never wanted to travel. **Read that last line again!** Our choices matter. Our decision to choose wisely can open and close doors and equip us for the unknowns and the unseens of life. They shape our view and predict our levels of devotion, determination, and the depth of our loyalty. The choices we make indicate our steadfast adherence to that which we claim allegiance. Our choices have the unique capability to enable us, paralyze us, as well as align us. Inevitably, choices define our beliefs, our morals, and our standards. Despite what we say, our actions always lead and actions always speak louder than our words. Our choices breathe life into our intentions. The choices we make are great predictors of achievement and disappointment, determining efficiency and highlighting potential. Our decisions can give sight to our blindness and wisdom to our ignorance. Never take the freedom of choice lightly. Choices are not trivial. No matter their size, they carry great weight.

If any of you lacks wisdom, let him ask God, who gives generously to all without reproach, and it will be given him. James 1:5 ESV

The fear of the Lord is the beginning of wisdom; all those who practice it have a good understanding. His praise endures forever! Psalm 111:10 ESV

For the Lord gives wisdom; from his mouth come knowledge and understanding; Proverbs 2:6 ESV

Blessed is the one who finds wisdom, and the one who gets understanding, Proverbs 3:13 ESV

There will be days we are faced with choices we would rather not make. We will not always feel like doing the right thing. We grow weary and tired of being the bigger person. We are exhausted from our failing attempts that never bring resolve. We are done with the whole "adulting" thing in general. I hear you! We must remember though - whatever we choose to focus on becomes magnified over everything else in our lives. Because of this truth, sometimes the very thing we are trying to avoid becomes the sounding alarm in our lives, becoming all that we can see or hear. Just like our raft on the Nantahala, we become stuck on the obstructions we focus on. We must learn to focus on where we are wanting to go instead of where we are because our feelings cast shade upon truth. Choosing to shift our focus does not negate our pain or discomfort. Choosing to shift our focus brings gentle rains of encouragement through humble obedience that reminds us there is something far greater at stake here.

Perhaps the greatest beauty of the gift of choice is the fact that it proves we are not bound up by a pre-determined plan for our lives. In His great love for us, God bestowed dignity upon us, enabling us to choose for ourselves. Although none of us have chosen to be born, we get to choose how we will live. Although we may not be able to choose all our circumstances, we can still choose our approach to, our reaction to, as well as our responses to our environment and culture. Even in the Garden of Eden, we see that Adam and Eve were given the gift of choice. Obedience and wisdom were never mandated with an iron fist. God was not standing over them with a whip in hand demanding they conform to His rules and standards.

If you love me, keep my commands.
John 14:15 NIV

l used to read this scripture from the perspective of a slave master cracking the whip down upon his slave while proclaiming, *"If you love me, then do as I say. If you really loved me, you would not continue to disobey and disrespect me. You must not love me at all."* Have you ever taken that stance with someone? I know I have. Our humanity can sometimes falsely lead us to believe that if someone truly loves us, they will not continue to disrespect us or cause us pain. This leads us to a place absent of grace, kindness, mercy, and forgiveness. My friend, this approach is from a human perspective of understanding love and relationships. God's angle is very different. This Scripture is one of a loving Father encouraging His child, *"If you love me with all your heart, don't worry about all this stuff because you will want to keep the boundaries outlined here. When you are in an authentic relationship with me, it will come as a desire of your heart to honor me with obedience. It will not be an 'I have to' mentality, but rather an 'I get to' mindset. I will help you. Just follow Me. Seek Me first."* In our freedom to choose we can find comfort in knowing that when we fall short, He is with us. God will help us stand back up and continue moving forward. The next part of this passage of scriptures says exactly that. We were given a Helper to guide us every day in making wise, healthy, and honorable choices in this journey called life.

See the difference between the two mindsets? Obedience and service will be the position of my heart when I am truly in love with, walking in relational awe and fear of, and seeking after God with all I am; with every part of my being. It is not a cracked whip coming down on my back telling me to straighten up and get in line, or else. In life, I have learned that I can refute, refuse, and reject what someone is speaking into and over my life. Likewise, I have the freedom to choose what I will say YES and NO to. I have been given the gift of an opportunity to align my heart with God, coming into agreement with His Kingdom and His will being brought to earth. And the beautiful truth is – so have you!

CHAPTER 10
PIGS IN THE KITCHEN

Have you ever found yourself completely overreacting and under-responding to a situation - yet, you could not stop yourself? If truthfully speaking, you did not want to stop yourself. The satisfaction of the justifiable reign of self-righteousness, as a result of the injustice you felt had been done to you, was undeniably bringing great joy in the moment. Injustice must be punished after all. Come on, I know I am not the only one. My Mom used to call this type of behavior *making mountains out of molehills*. I have been guilty many times of becoming my own mastermind. When I do this, I amplify the situation instead of appropriately moderating and managing the disappointment. Inevitably this leads to a bursting apart - much like the seams on the pants I recently tried to force myself into. I imagine many of us ladies have done this. Like a fly on the wall, we see ourselves from a distance, yet hardly recognize ourselves. This could not possibly be us. There is no way. Yet, there we are with all our glory and splendor on full display. Despite how "put together" we think we are; we do not have it all together by any stretch of the imagination. This person we see, well, she is ridiculous, unreasonable, and irrational – and that's candy-coating it!

    I never knew what a molehill was growing up, but if my Mom said it once, she said it a million times. Relatively small mounds of dirt left behind by burrowing animals are signs that something is going on beneath the surface that otherwise we would not necessarily know about. Although the sentiment of making mountains out of molehills is that of a person making a big deal out of something that needs to be overlooked, it is also true that molehills can be an indicator of a much larger issue at hand - something burrowing beneath the surface that needs to be dealt with! With that in mind, molehills and tunnels caused by moles and other burrowing animals can cause significant damage to your yard when ignored. I would not advise ignoring these pesky little varmints. When left unaddressed they will destroy what was once beautiful and alive, leaving mounds of dirt and tunnels in a once vibrantly healthy space. The same is true of the molehills of life. When they are left unattended and unaddressed, these imposters will cause substantial, and sometimes irreversible damage to our lives, our relationships, our finances, and our spirits.

Life is filled with moments when we realize that something much deeper is going on. Something is burrowing beneath the surface and in the process of destroying our space and peace. Remember that time when you cried because two socks went into the dryer and only one came out? That is most definitely a mound of dirt indicating a much deeper issue. They were your favorite "choose joy" socks too. How will you ever choose joy now that your "choose joy" socks have been stolen? It is so unfair. I must admit I sometimes think there is a conspiracy, a secret plot between the dryer companies and sock manufacturers.

One afternoon a few years ago the consistency of the strawberry frosting I was making turned out way too thin. My response? Toss it onto the floor – all of it. I wish I were joking, but I am not. Exhaling in deep and dramatic sighs of undeserved agony, I made my inflated and larger-than-life exit to take a bath – leaving my husband dumbfounded and scratching his head. Later I went to purchase a strawberry cake from the local bakery for the friend I had promised the cake to. On another occasion, I had once again overbooked myself to the point that I could not seem to figure out what should be done first. So, I did the most logical thing - nothing. In fact, I went shopping, with money we didn't have, instead. Overwhelmed, ignoring the elephant in the room (or the burrowing mole) seemed to be the best approach for conquering it!

Yes, yours truly is somewhat of a special intellect at times. I sometimes become irrational and unmotivated when I become overwhelmed. When I allow my schedule to become too crowded, I begin to suffer emotionally, mentally, spiritually, and physically. I have come to realize that any time I feel rushed, peace exits stage left. One way to make sure I don't feel rushed is to make sure I don't take on too much. I don't know why, but what I think I can accomplish and what I actually am able to accomplish in a single day are markedly different. It is hard to say no when someone is needing our assistance. It somehow makes us feel as if we are being bad Christians, women, friends, mothers, and leaders if we say no to someone. We get branded as not being a team player or being too rigid and not flexible enough. I know we band of sisters understand this! It is hard to be like Nehemiah, proclaiming that we cannot come down from the work we are doing. My natural bent is to be far too concerned with what others will think of me if I do not rise to meet their expectations and request. Often, I cross over the parameters that have been put in place to guard my sanity, trying to rise to every occasion on all occasions. The truth of the matter is this - I am one person and I cannot be everything to everyone in every season of life. A friend of mine once said it like this, "Someone else's poor planning is not my emergency." There will be times in life that require flexibility, but if we are walking in sync with God, then His interruptions will not cause chaos and stress in our lives. Anytime we are not walking in peace we need to take inventory.

One day while listening to Pastor Craig Groeschel on YouTube, the lightbulb finally went off in my head! I must let go of some things in the here and now to grab ahold of what is best; to take hold of my dreams and what I want most in life. Just because I can do something does not mean I should be doing it. Just because I am good at something does not mean I should allow it to consume my time and my life. Just because I say no to something or someone does not mean that I am a bad person. It does however mean that I am a focused person with healthy boundaries in place. It means that I have identified what must have my undivided attention during this season of life, and I'm pursuing that.

It is easy to say no when it is something we don't care much about, or when it's a situation we'd rather have a good excuse to avoid anyway. But, what about those moments we really enjoy? What about the hobbies we love? What about the friends we love hanging out with? What about the TV shows we get sucked into? Here is one that hits close to home - what about all the serving and ministry opportunities that are abundantly present in our everyday lives? They are good things after all. I have learned there will always be good things to be a part of. Just because something is a good thing does not mean it is the God thing for this season of my life. I must filter it through the lens of what I want most.

Recently I found myself filled with anxiety, once again; the kind of unease and unsettledness that leaves your heart racing inside your chest. I found making simple choices, such as whether or not I wanted creamer in my coffee, to simply be "too much." This unsettling angst is something I had not experienced for quite some time. Over the course of the previous six months though I had allowed little foxes to come in and spoil my realm of peace. These little foxes, as beautiful and enticing as they were, distracted me from God's best for me during this season of life. Slowly my schedule had gotten more and more packed, as before. Little by little I gave a YES when I should have said NO, or before I prayed and asked God what He wanted. As a result, I over-extended myself and chose something I enjoyed now over something I wanted most that had meaning, purpose, and destiny attached to it (Thank you Craig Groeschel for this incredible revelation as well). The straw that broke the legendary camel's back came at 5:25 am on the 3rd day of our church's annual 21-days of prayer. Standing in the kitchen preparing to leave for the 6:00 am corporate prayer, it hit me like a ton of bricks. All at once I broke. I could not process my emotions, much less find words to describe to my husband why I was shaking and feeling a panic attack coming down the pipe. The pressures of trying to be compassionate and gracious in a particularly difficult season of life, while at the same time maintaining healthy boundaries and not becoming a "yes girl" for the sake of avoiding an argument, became the last weight my scrawny little shoulders could manage to hold up. I had become self-sufficient once again because I had been steadily allowing opportunities, hobbies, expectations of others, and busy-task not attached to my purpose to creep back in. The problem is my self-reliance and sustainability efforts have gotten me nowhere in the past. You would think a girl would learn. You would think. That morning during prayer God spoke to me. He did not shout at me. He did not shame me. He did not point His fingers with an *"I told you so,"* kind of attitude. He whispered as a loving Father would to my overwhelmed heart,

There will always be good things to be a part of. There will always be good things you enjoy doing because I have given you desires and talents. The question is this though - are they the God things for this season of your life? In order to accomplish what you really want to do Valerie, and what I have called you to do, you must let go of the good things and grab ahold of the God things. You must let go of some of the things you enjoy for things that will bring the fulfillment of purpose and destiny.

WOW! It was not an audible voice. It was a soft whisper into my aching spirit. A gentle reminder. A gentle course correction. I felt seen by God himself. I felt understood too.

I knew the moment my husband and I were fighting on a Sunday morning about bacon and baked beans, that it was no longer about the bacon and baked beans. But for poor Pete's sake, what was this about? Seriously, who gets into a face-off and gets their feelers hurt over bacon and baked beans? Guilty as charged. Right here! Hi there!

There we stood head-to-head in a pork duel in the middle of our newly renovated kitchen. Nostrils flared and huffing ensued, not to be misread as hugging – there most definitely was not any hugging going on. The unveiling of the iconic head tilt and eye-rolling made its debut as the stage was set with defensiveness and misunderstanding on every front. We both became combative and the fangs came out. The scene was made complete with a poetically declared "WOW," as I exited the kitchen. I seem to be pretty good at dramatic exaltations and exits. It was a grand exit too, might I add! My school and church drama teachers would have been very proud! My husband announced he was going to church. They say hindsight is 20/20, whoever "they" may be – and in hindsight, I realize I should have followed suit. As an usher, Tommy needs to arrive an hour earlier than me to prepare the church auditorium for service. Because of this, most Sundays we drive separate vehicles – so this in and of itself was not unusual.

In the divinity of the Book of Val, I decided my best response would be to skip church altogether and go shopping instead. Super spiritual – I know. God already spanked me. As I journeyed out the door to Big Lots, I realized the car gas meter was showing I had a whopping 47 miles left till empty. I am a faith gal so this would be plenty of gas to get me there and back home. It was far too cold to stop for gas anyway. After all, Tommy could take care of that the following morning on his way to work. This, of course, is the part of the story where I fail to consider the stinging fact that he leaves the house between 3:45 am and 4:15 am every morning. At Big Lots, I found my lip gloss, which I had told myself was all I was going to get, along with a plethora of bathroom toiletry items, a teapot, a sheet set, a decorative wooden box, a large wall clock that matched nothing in my home, another blanket throw *(as if I needed another),* a pair of pants, two unicorn onesies for the oldest grandbabies, along with a buggy full of other completely random items of choice. No judging. I know I am not the only one who has ever embarked upon a budget-busting retail therapy excursion. That day I chose to drown my sorrows in the isles of the local Big Lots.

I returned home to find the hubs asleep on the couch. This made me angry. How could he be sleeping? I had been anticipating a text or call from him all morning as to my whereabouts, as well as with an apology. Yet, nothing. Nada. Silence. The nerve of him. I went about my business putting away all my purchases, hung my new wall clock *(that did not match anything),* made a cup of coffee, and then sat down at the computer to work on a project. Developing creative ideas and getting my vision to make sense on paper was not coming easily however. There was a huge creativity block. It seemed like I had sat there for hours - which was probably more realistically around 30 minutes. I knew at some point that Tom and I were going to need to talk this out. The kids were coming for lunch in about an hour and we were both ignoring the elephant in the room, or should I say – the proverbial pig in the room.

Have you ever watched a pig eat? They digest their food slowly, taking pleasure in and savoring the taste. Pigs also love a good mud bath, mainly because it helps them to cool their bodies in extreme heat *(I wonder if taking a mud bath would cool my body during this season of peri-menopause?).* It also plays a role in helping them rid themselves of pesky parasites that infest their bodies. Believe it or not, playing in the mud is also a way that pigs mark their territory. I had no choice but to acknowledge this pig in our home that was slowly enjoying and savoring its tasty meal of our peace, joy, and laughter. This pig was marking its territory through the legal access granted through stinking attitudes and hurt feelings. The wallowing mud pit in my kitchen was leaving a complete mess in our tidy home and hearts. There were definitely some pesky little parasites in attendance as well that needed to go! This pig and this mud pit were not about to mark our home, our hearts, and our marriage as its territory.

At some point during my deep self-reflection, careful articulation, and assessment of the issue at hand, my husband walked in and handed me a small black bag from McNair Jewelers off Broad Street. This small-town jewelry store is where we always take my wedding band set to be cleaned and the setting checked. I had noticed a few days prior the prong on one side of my ring seemed to be bent and so Tom had taken it in for me while I was teaching a cookie decorating class. He walked out of the room without a word and I slowly closed the laptop and begin to unwrap my very unexpected, and might I add underserved, gift. Inside I found a small black box that held a tiny pair of dainty gold cross earrings. They were beautiful. I am sure they had been meant for Valentine's Day, which was only a few days away, but he felt the need to go ahead and give them to me. Giving gifts is one of the ways he shows love.

A cross is a representation of the ultimate gift. It is a symbol of hope, reconciliation, and sacrifice. A cross reflects love in a collision of heaven kissing earth. The cross, therefore, renders all opposing antagonistic adversaries powerless. My husband just handed me love, hope, redemption, and reconciliation in a box. Me? I had nothing! I was speechless, which does not happen often! Believe me! Without saying anything he sacrificed his right to argue and prove his point. He saw the bigger picture. It wasn't about who was right and who was wrong. We are one. We are a team. If one of us loses, we both lose. I could choose to list out all the reasons I felt misunderstood, misjudged, and invisible. I could present my case, supported by all the necessary documentation and proof to clearly show reasonable cause and just reason for my feelings, as well as why baked beans need bacon. And I might be right. Likewise, Tommy could choose to list out all the reasons he felt the way he did. And he might be right as well. There is a delicate balance and narrow path we choose to walk every single day. It is a path of love and grace in the war for our hearts and souls. When we choose to stop fighting for our rightness and start seeking to understand instead of being understood, we will begin to experience breakthrough in our lives.

When the pig, the parasites, and the mud pit are identified and called out, a new lens is available through which to view the entire situation. The facts are no longer the priority. While facts may represent reality, facts are never good indicators of truth! When feelings and emotions no longer lead the pact, we can open ourselves to be led by the power of the Holy Spirit. Choosing to view the situation through a different lens enables us to see what perhaps could not be seen previously. We were able to see we were both exhausted, my husband's body was fatigued from a two-year fight with his health, we were both emotional over upcoming decisions we were needing to make regarding our future and our family, we both held onto unrealistic expectations of the other, and we had not been clearly communicating for a while due to our exhaustion. Mounds of dirt were everywhere indicating a deeper issue, but we had not seen them. We were dealing with my Dad's extreme health decline, Tom's Grandpa's health concerns, as well as the growing concerns with his Mom's health. Additionally, we were feeling the financial crunch of the added weight of medical bills and an ever-increasing cost of living that had been trying to place a chokehold on our sense of security and well-being. We had become tired and overwhelmed, drifting along on auto-pilot. This is how bacon and baked beans can lead to pigs and mud pits in the kitchen.

In 2018 Tom and I made a decision to live a life of surrender. This decision would not automatically mean we would get it correct one hundred percent of the time. It did mean that when we were faced with opposition, we already knew what to do because we decided years ago what our response would be. *(Thank you to Craig Groeschel, once again, for this incredible insight and wisdom.)* It was because we had decided to live a life of surrender that we were both able to ask God to show us what the real issue was. There was a time in our lives (you read about earlier) a misunderstanding like this would have led to weeks of silence and punishment of one another. Now, because of this commitment of surrender and resolve, we were able to remove the blinders and see that the enemy was trying to attack in moments of weakness - true to his nature of course. Through a pre-established plan to choose to surrender every day, we were able to recognize that perhaps we both needed to sharpen our communication skills, while at the same time remembering to extend grace. We also needed to prioritize sleep and rest. We are both on the same team. We are not at war with one another. We are at war FOR one another. We are each other's biggest cheerleaders and fans! We are not enemies, and most certainly, we are not in a face-to-face pork duel. We are in a life battle and we need one another.

It was not about bacon and baked beans – it never was! God had revealed a molehill in our life that needed our immediate attention before it destroyed everything. This was about those cross earrings. What a beautiful reminder of my Father's love given to me through my husband. It is a beautiful reminder that my Father's love leaves the ninety-nine to find the one. It is also a beautiful reminder of a love that watches over the ninety-nine while searching for the one. My Father's love cannot be worked for or earned as if it were wages – It is a gift to receive and to reciprocate. My Father's love is unlike any human love I have ever known. His love is always patient, loving, kind, generous, giving, selfless, and hard-focused on my heart. It is not scheming, demanding, manipulative, harsh, difficult, self-seeking, or hard to satisfy. It is complete, thorough, absolute, and downright excessive – and I am bankrupt without it. His love is a stone in my slingshot of faith, wind on my back, sun on my face, and breath in my lungs. His love is furious and ferocious, fighting battles for me – like pigs that find their way into my kitchen.

CHAPTER 11
HEALTHY BOUNDARIES

Recently the sweetest couple purchased the land beside our home and built the most adorable modern farmhouse. I love all things modern and traditional farmhouse style. Tom and I had previously looked at the property and considered purchasing for the land to eventually build a shop. After our due diligence in comparing the financial commitment with our future goals (what we wanted most in life), and time spent in prayer, we decided it was not a decision we wanted to move forward with. At the time we had zero debt other than our home, and we desired to pay that off as quickly as possible so we could enjoy our retirement years. Going further into debt did not make sense to us based on our future goals.

Throughout the entire building process, Pam and Tim kept us informed, always generous in their consideration to make sure we were not bothered or put out in any way. They planned to live in their camper on the backside of the property while their new home was being constructed. Before new construction could begin, however, the existing decaying old farmhouse and barn had to be torn down and cleared away. This old farmhouse and barn had served as an icon for years to those in our community, often used as a navigational marker when giving directions to others. The memories of yesteryear were framed in the iconic honor-system vegetable and firewood stand on the corner of the property with a locked money box. Tom and I often frequented the stand to purchase whatever goodies were available seasonally.

We could not have mail-ordered custom designed better neighbors than Pam and Tim. When they go out of town, they make sure we have their garage code in case a storm comes and we need to access their storm-safe room. This is certainly way more desirable than crawling underneath our house to access the designated area beneath the front porch steps that has been deemed as our "safe room." For some reason my knees and back spring into full-blown rejection and retaliation at even the slightest thought of this; not to mention all the creepy crawly things that can lurk beneath a home. Do not get me wrong - I am an outdoorsy girl who loves hiking in nature, but without a doubt, I can confidently verify to you that I am not an underneath-the-house kind of girl. Nope! Unquestionably, I hope to install our very own safe room or storm shelter at some point in the future. Until then I am grateful for our incredible neighbors offering to share theirs with us!

I recall one trip my husband and I took where we forgot to ask one of the neighbors if they would pull our trashcan to the road. It was filled to the brim with stinky yuckiness. Our oversight hit me of course too late and I pondered the rest of the trip on what we would do with the new trash until the can with the current stinky trash could be emptied on the next trash pickup day. I could just imagine the aroma rising from the can by this point, as well as how intensely fragrant it would be after another week. We arrived home to discover our neighbors had our back. They had noticed our can and pulled it to the road for us on trash day, while also watching for any packages that may have arrived so they could place them in a safe place until our return. Everyone needs neighbors like we have. We are surrounded on every side by generous, thoughtful, caring, and giving neighbors whom we also get the pleasure of calling friends.

Confirming property boundary lines before the purchase of land or a home is of great importance. A lot of work, money, and effort goes into surveying and clearly defining property lines that can sometimes seem to stall out the progress of moving forward. However, failure to clearly define property lines can cause a huge headache down the road. I also recall Pam and Tim waiting for what seemed to be an eternity for their foundation to be ready and for the framework to go up. Failure to lay a proper foundation for a new home can cause huge stability and infrastructure problems years down the road; complications that may not be visible right away. The patience and attention to detail on the front end will insure and protect you from future stresses, issues, concerns, disputes, and anxieties down the road. I remember the day their house was completed and they could finally move in. They had been living in that camper for far too long and their new home was a breath of fresh air. Now they enjoy mornings sipping coffee and watching the sunrise on their back patio instead of in a yard chair on fake grass outside their camper.

The same is true with personal boundaries and foundations. Our personal boundaries inherently define who we are. These personal boundaries are foundational to our life and are no different from the property lines of our homes. They mark our life's contours, shapes, and configurations. Personal boundaries define what we will and will not conform to and shed light upon our alignments. It is upon these boundary lines that our lives are erected. Properly defining what those boundaries are from the beginning will help circumvent much distress and misunderstanding down the road. The boundaries I implement in my life speak about what I value, what I believe, and what my needs are, but they also define who I am not. These boundaries outline specifically what I will not allow in my life.

When we implement healthy boundaries, we have a greater capacity to love and respect others. These boundaries strengthen our ability to extend to others that which God has so freely given to us. I love when Lysa TerKeurst says that boundaries are God's idea - because they are! God introduced and implemented boundaries with His creation from the very beginning. He modeled this perfectly as He spoke our world into existence, introducing the concept that boundaries are necessary, healthy, and for our protection. A life lived without boundaries is a life lived on impulse, on a whim, and carelessly. What if there were no boundaries placed upon the seas or the skies? Can you imagine? Just like children find security and a sense of well-being within the protective limitations their parents impose, the same is true for us – boundaries provide a fortress for our lives that shelter and safeguard us. Like our earth, life too must have guardrails and margins. Boundaries breed peace and demolish chaos. The limitations set forth by boundaries are not designed to be harmful or restrictive by a harsh God in Heaven aiming to inoculate mankind with fear, but rather by a loving Father who longs for his children to experience the freeing properties that boundaries bring.

I have spent a huge portion of my life caring more about the opinion of man than the opinion of God. This was not done consciously or purposely, but rather through my inaction and inattentiveness. Because of the overwhelming addiction I had of wanting to be accepted and liked, I did not draw healthy boundary lines that would protect me. The funny thing about respect is that we generally must give it to receive it. That means I can never expect respect and compliance from others on invisible boundary lines I have not drawn or respected myself. Choosing to respect and honor my heart, as well as the convictions God had placed within me, made requiring that same level of respect and compliance from others easier to implement and demand. This is what clearly defining the boundary lines looks like. It is a beautiful picture of love. God himself has drawn a boundary line that cannot be crossed. He demands respect of this boundary. Sin separates us from God. Sin cannot cross the barrier. Only the atonement can bridge the chasm and close the divide. There is no compromise because sin cannot co-exist with God.

For years I had a faulty understanding of what being a peace-maker was and therefore constantly caved and conceded. In hindsight, I can see my entire life played out as one big harmonious dance of negotiations and compromise – all in the name of acceptance and keeping the peace. I would go a hundred miles out of my way and bend over backward if it meant avoiding a conflict or drama, instead of standing firm on my convictions and laying life's stresses and concerns at the foot of the cross. My entire life I watched as my Mom disappeared further and further into the backdrop, becoming invisible and disposable by others because she refused to draw healthy boundary lines. My mom is one of the most beautiful spirits, but so often misunderstood by others. Truth is, she simply did not know how to draw healthy boundary lines because of her disordered and extremely destructive upbringing. She was always left feeling just short of acceptable. For me, I thought that keeping the peace was the same as being a peacekeeper, and I'm here to set the record straight. IT IS NOT! Keeping the peace often includes becoming a doormat. As a child of God, I am His heir. I am a daughter of the one and only true King of Kings and Lord of all Lords! I was never created to be a doormat for others to walk on. I am the only one who can permit people to walk on me. Allowing others to walk on me does not make me some sort of holy martyr either. There is a fine line between turning the other cheek and becoming a doormat. This line has often been crossed, blurred, ignored, or altogether become unrecognizable.

    I regularly entered into arbitration and came into agreement with that which was less than best for me because of my faulty understanding and belief system. This tolerance for compromise and refusal to acknowledge my own heart and guard it became like a tsunami wave rippling across the shores of my life, making its destructive path wide and deep as it rushed inland. The unintended impact and outcome became devastating in my life. Satan knew this about me long before the scales ever fell from my eyes. He was hard at work before I even knew what hit me. There I was, pummeled by the sheer force of the wave, bleeding on a heap of the nothingness called life. We must understand that what we feel will lie to us! We are designed to be led by the Holy Spirit, not by our soulish man and emotions. Emotions are not wrong, they are designed by God and given to us as a gift. However, how we steward the gift of emotions is completely upon our shoulders. We get to choose whether or not we will be ruled by our feelings, or if we will rule our feelings - allowing the Spirit of God to order our steps daily. If we allow our feelings to take the lead, we will eventually find ourselves worn out and exhausted. We must be okay with not being accepted by all and included in every circle. We must be okay with taking a stand for ourselves, our beliefs, and our convictions. Additionally, we must understand that we will be misunderstood at times, even by those we love the most - sometimes especially by those we love the most. Recognition of this fact - that the desire for acceptance and approval of man has little gain eternally - will lift a huge weight from your shoulders. Trust me, this I know to be the truth!

    Not all will see or give grace for that which you grieve, whether you are grieving the living, the dead, or something else in life. Some will not extend to you the gift and grace of a season to grieve at all. Not all will see the tireless hours of input and effort behind the scene, and therefore, will assume wrongful opinions of your contribution and position. Sometimes they will even voice this opinion in a passive/aggressive format. Some will expect compliance with "rules" that were never communicated. Not all will include you, yet still place unrealistic expectations upon you. Not all will extend a benefit of the doubt to you, and will wrongfully heap their judgment upon you. Some will seek to manipulate and control you through intimidation or manipulation. Others will seek to include you only when they can control you, or when it is convenient for them. Read that last line again and allow it to sink in for a moment. We live in one of the most narcissistic generations that has ever existed. We are born with an essential and inherent need and longing for inclusion and connectivity, a longing that seemingly fades into the backdrop of life as the world we live in seeks to program us for separateness and individuality. We live in a culture that is self-focused more than others-focused. This breeds insecurity that gives birth to narcissistic behavior, conceit, and self-absorption – behavior patterns we are all subject to and prone to if we do not implement and adhere to healthy boundary lines. Implementing healthy boundaries is made possible by prioritizing the presence of God every day in our lives.

While it is true, we are to be a people of peace, the same is true that we were never called to sacrifice our peace on the altar of another's ego! As long as it is possible, we should live in peace and at peace, but we should never allow the dismissing actions of others to root inside us. This weapon of the enemy is designed to breed insecurity about promise, purpose, and destiny. It stifles and suffocates the fire God is fanning to flame within us. Understanding a lack of respecting boundaries is more about who "they" are than it is about who "we" are is powerful in gaining the courage to implement healthy boundaries! Other's controlling and manipulative behaviors will seek to rewrite our God-ingrained identity. Listen to me for a minute and hear me - You are enough! You are not too much and you are not deficient. You and I were created in the image of God to bare His likeness. God created us by design with a specific purpose to make a difference and impact in this place called earth! Since we are created in the likeness of our Father, we are called to implement boundaries that cannot be crossed. This is a beautiful gift of protection God has equipped us with. God is not a doormat in the name of acceptance and peace, therefore – neither should we be!

While we are always seeking towards pursuing God and aligning our hearts and lives with Him, we can be certain there will be attacks along this path. We must remember, however, that everyone is on a path and strolling along at different paces. This path of sanctification looks different for everyone. Be sure to extend grace! Be sure to speak kindness in truth that is wrapped in love. Satan will use anyone and stop at nothing to render God's children ineffective, including us. Do not allow yourself to become a tool in his arsenal to be used against others in a quest to defend your boundaries. Stand firm in kindness while being confidently and firmly planted in beliefs, convictions, and principles. Remember, we are called up higher. We are called to rise above the noise and distractions. We are not called to become entangled in that which was launched to drive us off course. We must remember that truth not spoken in love and with grace is just meanness. I saw a beautiful fall picture on Facebook today. The winding road that ran along the shoreline was engulfed in trees that were every shade of the rainbow. I could imagine the Hubbs and me riding the Harley along the coastline and taking in this picture-perfect scape. Then I realized that on the same level as the road, I would never be able to see the entire scope of beauty that I could see from the overhead picture. Sometimes it is only by rising above something that we can see the full picture and appreciate its beauty and purpose.

We cannot fight against unknown battles with unknown and invisible enemies. Expose the enemy and his lies. Recognizing the culprit is only half the battle though. Keep in mind we are not at war against flesh and blood. Broken people break other people. If you are continually having venom spewed at you, draw a healthy boundary line. Boundaries are designed to offer a safe space, so never apologize for boundaries you implement, but rather stand firm on them. You can still love with healthy boundaries in place. Sometimes it is better to love from a distance for a season. It is not a "my way or the highway" type of approach, lest we become manipulative ourselves. There is a fine line. The benefits of choosing to guard our hearts and minds in Christ advances the peace of God in our lives; it's a place where the peace of God stands as a militant defense. It is a place where chaos cannot enter. It is a place accessible through the discernment and wisdom we receive through the Holy Spirit. Be gracious, but do not be fearful to draw lines. Be honorable and respectful, and be sure to practice the pause. Be slow to speak so you have time to meditate and seek God. This will slow you down, allowing you to be proactive instead of reactive. Listen. Hear. Only then, speak - but speak firmly with tenderness. Boundaries will help us understand and navigate life. They will help our YES be YES and our NO be NO. Boundaries will guide, protect, and provide a margin for the overstepping and error of others.

There are a few honorable mentions about boundaries that I think are worth bringing up. These are boundaries that God has revealed to me that have made a world of difference in my day-to-day life. They have ushered in peace and created space for God to cultivate His calling within me.

- **Our clearly defined and articulated boundaries will always adhere to the life code that one will reap what they sew.** This is a God principle and law both in nature, as well as in our lives. I would never expect to harvest from an orange tree if I planted an apple seed. That may seem silly at first but think about this concept for a moment. I can think back to several instances across the span of my life where I anticipated a harvest from something I did not plant or make a deposit towards. There are indeed occasions dotted throughout the historical timeline where God chose to bless His children bountifully out of His goodness and His nature, instead of their inattentiveness to the importance of tilling, planting, tending, and waiting in expectation; instances where He chose to bless His children without their painful toil for it. However, it is more so than not that the opposite stands fixed. The propensity and tendency of the culture we live in is one bent towards entitlement; the expectation of rewards viewed as privilege, justice, and laid claims for something one did not work towards or earn. Our lives are a direct reflection of the choices and decisions we make daily. We cannot live only for ourselves and expect others to come running when we need them. We cannot spend like there is no tomorrow and wonder what happened when tomorrow comes. We cannot live an unassumed life of self-focused agendas and expect the bounty that close personal relationships enrich life with. We cannot expect peace if we constantly blur the lines and allow chaos entrance.

- **Our clearly defined and articulated boundaries speak of another truth - actions speak louder than words.** I heard this statement more times than I care to remember growing up. The simple reality is that this tiny little phrase is power-packed with enormous truth and life application! This is a truth we must enforce and adhere strongly to with our healthy boundaries. If someone tells me daily that they love me, yet they never call unless they need something from me, it might leave me feeling deprived and lonely. Relationships fill our lives with joy, purpose, and meaning, while simultaneously holding the power to drain the very lifeblood from our veins. Unhealthy relationships can easily become one-sided if one party is more intentional and focused than the other. Unhealthy relationships hold one party at a distance and only seek what they can gain from the connection.

What does this look like in real-life practical application? I am glad you asked. Raising our son Eli was not a task for the light-hearted. It took a deep love laced with tough and consistently monitored boundary lines. Constant maintenance of these boundary lines was required to ensure there were no ruptures or cracks. The teenage Eli was a master at finding a weak link and picking at it until it became a gaping hole in the wall. By the time it became a gaping hole my defenses were usually fatigued, my spirit exasperated, and my physical body longing for retreat. In this condition, it became easier to bend and compromise for the sake of some sort of a resemblance of peace. I had no doubt Eli loved us; however, he understood and defined love very differently than we did. This is important to recognize. We do not war against flesh and blood. Another's inability to contribute to the sustainability of a healthy relationship does not equate to their overall worth as a human. They are still God's child made in His image. With this truth in mind, I had to realize that although Eli often desired to do what was right, he would more often end up making choices and decisions that were damaging and destructive. He had a fleshly natural bent towards dishonesty, manipulation, violence, abuse, selfishness, theft, lying, and maneuvering situations and circumstances to meet his needs. Like a switch being flipped, he could go from one to ten in the blink of an eye – with no in-between. This will cause a person to stay in a constant state of fight or flight. The guard is always up. You are always peering around the next corner. Your sleep is never restful as you are constantly awaiting the next explosion. You know it is not a matter of if, but when that explosion will occur. It was not until 2013 that I began to recognize the great need for healthy boundaries to be implemented, but it would take many years to fully be able to take a stand on demanding respect for those boundaries from my son. Drawing this healthy boundary line with Eli opened the door for God's peace to stand guard over my heart. I had to realize that despite what Eli's words were, I always had to look at his actions and life patterns that followed. Allowing a breech in the healthy boundary lines I had drawn would cause an unintended, and yet very unwelcomed ripple effect in my life that I was not willing to allow anymore. I could no longer sacrifice my spiritual, mental, financial, and physical health on this altar. There had to be zero tolerance for non-compliance if I were to maintain my health. I know my son loves me and Tommy. I know he loves our family, but words alone are never enough. The actions of one person can bring destruction, lack, and curses to an entire bloodline. Learning to love from a distance is not fun. Grieving the living does not come with a "how-to" little rule book. Grief is most often messy and painful, ricocheting and trying its best to rebound. In instances such as this, you learn to stand firm, keep your focus fixed, and often remind yourself that boundaries are God's idea and for our protection and His glory! (Thank you Lysa TerKeurst for this revelation that has radically transformed my life!)

- **Our clearly defined and articulated boundaries build character and confidence.** They annihilate unwarranted guilt. When we have the courage to stand by our convictions, despite the opinions, the sentiments, and the unsolicited input often received from others, we bring clarity to the very qualities that are distinctive to our core identity. Our disposition strengthens and enforces our declaration by diminishing our flexibility in this area. Flexibility in relationships is often considered to be a good quality, that is unless we are talking about healthy boundary lines, in which case we need to be resolute in our stance. We cannot waver, give in, or bend under the pressure of others. Satan loves to place unjustified guilt upon us when we feel judged by others for standing firm on our boundaries. Our ability to recognize his tactics will enable us to tackle the enemy head-on and thereby avoid potential threats to our position of peace.

- **Our clearly defined and articulated boundaries are support beams for a healthy life.** One of the best decisions we can ever make for ourselves is to make ourselves a matter of importance. Okay, you probably already know what I am about to say – go back and read that last statement one more time. Now, stop and think about it for a moment. We often hear about prioritizing

God in our lives, but have you ever considered that God wants us to prioritize ourselves as well? Lean in and allow me to whisper something to your soul - He does! Not only does God want us to make ourselves a matter of importance, but it is also not selfish to do so. We are called to steward our bodies (temple) well.

One of my favorite hashtags I have been using on social media is #BecauseIMatter. There is a wealth of truth in this. Our lives are crazy. Our crazy is even crazy. My eyes spin most mornings when I look at the ever-growing and never-ending to-do list on my calendar. Sometimes I feel I need to schedule potty breaks just to make sure I don't wait too late. That's insane! There comes a time when intervention becomes necessary. Marking out healthy boundary lines as it relates to diet, lifestyle, physical activity, emotional health, spiritual health, and relational health is paramount to a life of abundance and peace. **If we are overly consumed by our busyness of doing the good works that we forgo the God works in our lives, then friends – we are simply too busy – perhaps even busier than God ever intended for us to be.** This is an area of my life that I often must reevaluate. Part of God's plan is for us to find purpose and make a difference. It is far easier to live out our purpose when we feel good and are not exhausted, or running on fumes. I once heard Pastor Rick Warren state if we are burning at both ends of the candle, perhaps we are not as bright as we think we are. Our bodies are the temple of the Lord and we are to treasure our bodies in their entirety, stewarding them well, so we can live authentically and intentionally, with urgency and vigor.

- **Our clearly defined and articulated boundaries can break generational curses and close the gap on unhealthy perpetuating cycles.** This will take courage and boldness, but I believe you can do it. With God's help, I have been able to identify the generational lines of depression, mental illness, disease, addictive behaviors, and financial hardships negatively impacting the generations of my family. I have watched as family members have all passed from the same disease far too soon. Food, drug, and alcohol addictions have robbed us more than we care to acknowledge. Depression has stolen years of joy, peace, and contentment. Mental illness has brought a destructive force that has left life unrecognizable at times. Learning to harness and couple the power of prayer with the audible and spoken word of God has been the predominant driving force in breaking these curses and unhealthy cycles off my life, as well as off of our family's lives. Learning to take an unashamed, defiant stand against an enemy who tries to intimidate through trespassing on anointed grounds takes brazenly bold courage. This courage only comes from time spent in the secret place with God. This is war, so suit up daily with the full armor of God. Don't go into battle unprepared.

There is more to this than just declaring the promises and praying the prayers though. This boundary line will require further action. Your entire bloodline depends upon the healthy boundaries you draw today. Future generations are dependent upon your courage. Draw a line in the sand and say – **NO MORE! ENOUGH IS ENOUGH!** I still remember the day I stood in the middle of the living room in my tiny apartment, staring at the ceiling and screaming – **WHEN WILL ENOUGH BE ENOUGH?** There can be no more compromise, no more tolerance, and no more allowance of anything unholy. No more entertaining that which is beneath the calling God has placed upon our lives. We must come to a place of no return where we know – it is now or never. Pray for forgiveness. Ask for clarity and guidance. Speak and believe the promises of the truth of God's word. Draw the line where it needs to be drawn. If food addiction is the problem, then recognize it for what it is and build a community of support around you. If alcohol is the problem, put action to your desires and build a community of support to help. If emotional spending is the problem, own it and put mechanisms in place that challenge that behavior every single time you feel tempted. If generational lifestyle and diet-related diseases are the issues, then start today on a new path. If looking at pornography is the issue, get accountability. If isolation is the natural bent you have, engage the support of a few friends that can keep watch for it swinging too far out of balance – draw the line! This in conjunction with powerful bondage-breaking prayers and the word of God will catapult you into a life of hope and promise. Do what is possible for you to do, then trust God to do that which only He can do. Our job is to send the word and trust. His job is the fulfillment of the word. You are worth every ounce of effort, every tear, and every step of the journey! You matter. You can do this. You can do the hard things!

- **Our clearly defined and articulated boundaries always speak the truth in love.** I have always believed that unless the truth is presented with kindness and dignity, it really is not much truth at all. I can still hear the words of my Momma ringing in my ears today, *"If you can't say something nice, then don't say anything at all."* We can communicate our boundaries and speak truth, but it should always be done in a manner that is considerate and kind to others. If we cannot love, we possess nothing of value. The very word itself speaks of the ability to be sincere, honest, and genuine. We accomplish very little if we win battles only to find we have lost the entire war. There is an old saying that we can catch more flies with honey than vinegar. When we season our speech with love, the light we are representing begins to add flavor to everything we touch. Everyone we encounter will notice. Draw the boundary line that keeps rudeness and selfishness at bay, and welcomes tenderness and empathy with open arms.

- **Our clearly defined and articulated boundaries communicate that it really is okay to say NO!** It is even ok if others do not agree or understand. Your YES to anything and anyone should always be passed through the hands of God first. So should your NO! Your response to anything should be aligned with what matters most in your life before giving any knee-jerk and unthought-out answer or response. Recently I was reading an amazing book written by Lysa TerKeurst (one of my favorite authors), *The Best Yes*, and immediately a million tiny shards of truth penetrated my heart. For the first time in my life, I felt empowered to stand firm on this boundary without fear of the repercussions of others. There may be times we will be called to draw a healthy boundary line across a road we want to cross. We must recognize that not all things are for all the seasons of our lives. A NO right now does not necessarily mean it will be a NO forever. Similarly, there may be times we are called to say YES when we would rather not. Drawing healthy boundary lines over our YES and NO will equip us to live balanced lives that bring about freedom and true rest. It will prevent us from over-extending ourselves. It will authorize the power of God to be unleashed into our lives.

These unforced rhythms of grace will echo through our lives and become the hallmark of our identity. Identifying and implementing these clearly defined boundaries bring about wisdom as we discern what is and is not right for us, standing firm in our convictions.

CHAPTER 12
ALL THE LITTLE DEBBIE CAKES
Understanding Generational Bondages and Strongholds

Gaining understanding of the assignment and commission of the generational bondages, curses, and pervasive strongholds in my life was precisely what Satan never wanted me to become aware of. What I believed in my heart, and whispered under my breath played out in my life. Even more disturbing would be the discovery of everything I was unaware of that was the driving force behind my reactions, choices, and behaviors. Everything in our lives has a root, and I am a roots girl! Understanding these roots is powerful in gaining complete freedom and living in peace. Let me encourage you to ask your parents and grandparents to share with you about their lives. Not only does it bring a bond that closely knits you together with them, but it will help you to understand and identify generational strongholds and curses within your family lineage.

Forewarning – this is a long chapter because there is so much to say about this topic.
Buckle Up and Hold On Tight!

"I'll eat all the Little Debbie Cakes I want." This is what the seven-year-old me declared as I walked around the left side of our split-level home my parents had built when I was three years old. I can still vividly remember almost everything about that

hot summer afternoon as I spoke a self-fulfilling prophecy over my life. I was very unhappy with being told I could not have another Little Debbie snack cake. Little Debbie snack cakes are in a league all their own, and snack cakes of any kind were a true treat in those days. We lived on a very tight budget and all sweets and desserts were closely monitored to prevent any from becoming "missing in action," if you know what I mean. If you have never tasted one of these little treats, you are certainly missing out on one of life's sweetest pleasures. Although I no longer partake in these jewels, I also cannot deny their addictive and enticing draw. I declared in my heart and with my lips that summer day that when I grew up, I would buy as many as I wanted, and eat as many as I wanted - every single day. No one would ever tell me I could not have a snack again. Furthermore, I also declared that when I had children that I would never deprive them of Little Debbie snack cakes.

I wish I could tell you this declaration served me well, but it did not. As innocent as it was, and as cute and unassuming as it may have seemed seeing a seven-year-old child make such a silly declaration, it was anything but innocuous. In a single ordinary moment of my ordinary life, a motion was set in place that would alter the trajectory of my relationship with food for years to come, as well as how my children would perceive a healthy relationship with food. Words are powerful and they absolutely, one thousand percent matter. The vows we make matter as well. Not only our vows to others and God, but also the vows we make to ourselves. Vows are oaths that sometimes can make declarations that undermine the God-ordained purposes that mark our lives. Corrupt vows are aimed at derailing our rationale and resoluteness. The enemy of our soul does not care what age we are. Satan does not fight fair or only pick on those his own size. We do not get a pass just because we don't realize the gravity and seriousness of what we are doing and saying.

When a baby is born, by design it bonds with its mother through the process of feeding. Food, serving as a connection point, brings a sense of love, attachment, warmth, belonging, comfort, support, and well-being. God designed us to connect and bond through the process of nurturing and feeding. It is nourishment to our bodies and our souls. As we grow older and wean from milk and our mothers, God purposed for us to continue finding connection in the context of relationships with others. God intended for us to live within a community where we could find strength, encouragement, inspiration, and joy while caring for one another and urging one another along the way. Living connected to others is not always easy though. Sometimes it is downright discouraging. I'm certain we have all experienced the difficulties of relational hardships that strain and complicate our lives. Sometimes it seems to be more work and effort than it's worth. Yet, we find time and time again throughout Scripture the urgency of God's call to live united; to help one another through the day-to-day ups and downs of life.

As a child, I never learned to connect with others very well outside of my parents, family, and close family relationships. Because my natural bent was to isolate myself, living in my little bubble of reality was my preference. I found life to be extremely uncomfortable when I was forced to interact with others, although I desired this interaction as I grew older. Although a part of me longed to be included, I still much preferred the seclusion and safety found within my own company. Because I never really developed a true sense of belonging within community, I continued to look outside of healthy relationships with others and my relationship with God for comfort, encouragement, peace, and fulfillment.

My parents worked very hard when my brother and I were growing up. They were determined to give us the life they never had. We never lacked anything we truly needed; however, we never had a lot of excess or fluff either. We were mostly always happy and felt a sense of safety and security. Mom and Dad often went without, making sure we had the life they had always longed for – a life well loved. Once I was old enough to attend school, I became very aware of the fact that we did not have as much as other kids in our school. Sure, there were those far worse off than we were, however, the other children seemed to think it was their sole purpose on earth to criticize my clothing, my shoes, my hair, my teeth, my appearance – pretty much everything about me. I was always left feeling just short of acceptable, just like my Mom did as a child. This was a generational bondage hiding in plain sight.

In second grade I recall a pair of velvet blue colonial vintage-style knee breeches I wore with my knee-high white socks. I can still see them in my mind when I close my eyes. I loved how the material felt against my skin, smooth and soft. You can probably imagine my disappointment to discover that my peers were poking fun at me behind my back because they did not admire my knee breeches nearly as much as I did. I think I felt a little like Dolly Parton in her little coat of many colors. My brother and I were recipients of the free and reduced-price breakfast and lunch programs at school for many years. This was a huge help to my parents. We also utilized green stamps, one of the earliest and first customer retail loyalty programs. The stamps were mostly distributed at our local grocery stores and gas stations. Once the booklets were filled, we cashed them in for treasures we could never have afforded otherwise. Collecting the stamps was exciting and always gave us something to look forward to. Recently my Mom gave me an old shoe box filled with leftover remnants of green stamp books and old green stamps. What a trip down memory lane as I rummaged through the contents of the old shoe box.

Momma told us stories of spending $10 a week on groceries for a family of four when we were little. This was before she went to work full-time. In today's economy that would be somewhere between $31-$41, depending on which online calculator you used. Can you imagine trying to feed your family for about $7-$10 per person, per week in today's economy? Every week the menu was mostly the same. Beans, potatoes, cornbread, oatmeal or grits, peanut butter, flour, milk from the local dairy where Daddy had struck up a deal, round butter cookies we wore as rings on our fingers, bread, and saltine crackers. Our food supply was supplemented with the annual garden Mom would plant as well. Occasionally there would be chicken, canned tuna, or a pot of Dad's homemade chili or goulash. Mom would also splurge on brown sugar to put on top of our oatmeal. She had grown up being forced to eat plain oatmeal (out of necessity) and to this day she cannot make herself eat oatmeal. I remember once waking up and coming downstairs to find her deep frying some breaded mushrooms. I had never experienced such deliciousness. That night she shared her special treat with me, which at the time I did not realize just how special that moment was.

These small simple acts of thoughtfulness from my Mom and Dad are dotted throughout my childhood and are memories that I will hold onto for a lifetime. I will forever be grateful for their love and support, and for their numerous sacrifices they made. It is easy to overlook the small acts of kindness and selfless acts of sacrifices from others, but I implore you to choose to remember. We can choose to think about kindness when negativity is bidding for precious real estate in our hearts and minds. I have heard it said and I agree – it is often the little things that are the biggest things.

Sunday lunches were enjoyed at Pate's Bait Shop, the bait and tackle shop my Little Mama and Daddy Cups owned and ran for years. I have many fond memories of Pate's Bait Shop located right smack dab on the direct route to what we called "the river." Although run down and in need of great repair, memories of yesteryear are still tucked away behind overgrown brush as you travel down Highway 47 to Shelby. Everyone stopped by Pates! I use to play in the minnow vats trying to see how many minnows I could scoop up at a time. We loved climbing on top of the roof, exploring in the woods behind the shop, and sitting out front shooting the breeze in the metal gliders and chairs. Pate's Bait Shop did not have indoor plumbing for bathroom facilities, so we grew up using an old-fashioned outhouse when visiting. It was a two-seater as well. Lucky us. Mom depended on that one meal a week being provided to make the food budget stretch until the next payday.

One particularly harsh and cold winter our Little Mama went to the local Western Auto in town to purchase electric blankets for my brother and me. We could not afford to heat our home to a comfortable temperature. We used the fireplace as much as possible to keep the main living areas warm, but at night the cold air would creep in. Mom and Dad had each other to keep warm, but my brother and I were still cold even with every available blanket in the house piled high on our beds. Our childhood would not have been complete without the infamous and iconic clothesline as well. Although we had an electric dryer in the basement, I remember Mom hanging all our clothes outside to save on electricity. We loved running through the clothes as they dried on the line, almost as much as we loved running and jumping into her piles of freshly raked leaves in the fall. It was a simple life I now see and appreciate the beauty of; a life I wish we could recapture. It is funny though – I did not realize it was a simple life at the time. It was the only life I knew.

My Mom grew up in extremely impoverished conditions. The poverty and abuse she experienced in life have in some ways marked her until this very day. Her disadvantaged status meant that she and her brothers often did not have access to health care, dental and vision care, adequate housing (at times living in homes with dirt floors and sleeping on pallets), or nutritious and regular meals. Her family often worked as field hands and lived in sub-par housing which would barely qualify as a shack – and would be condemned by today's standards most certainly. My Mamaw chopped cotton by hand from 6:00 am until 6:00 pm for $3 a day when my Mom was a little girl. Mom suffered permanent damage to her feet due to wearing shoes that were too tight. Mom's father, Leeman, was a harsh man who suffered with alcohol addiction and undiagnosed mental illness. He died when I was only three months old so I never had the opportunity to know him. The alcohol made him abusive, many times taking out his frustrations and anger on his wife and children.

    Mom tells of a vivid memory she has where her dad rubbed her nose in pee because she had wet the bed, once again. This, and other methods of severe dehumanizing punishment, were the norm for my Mom growing up. Often my Grandpa would send the children to bed hungry, only to then have my Mamaw cook him a steak he had bought on the way home. Mom and her brothers would lay in bed smelling the steak with their tummies growling.

Mamaw was not allowed to eat any of it either, and she dared not refuse to cook it for him or else she would suffer the consequences. Sometimes he would give them a dime to walk to the store for candy, a rare treat, and then pull out a steak for Mamaw to cook for him. It was normal for my Mom and her siblings to live in a community long enough for bills to be run up and the paychecks to be drunk away. Then they would be moved to the next town where my grandpa could find work - this perpetuating cycle played over and over in her life.

My Mom's very first memory of life came when she was only two years old. Some may say that is too early to have clear memories, but my Momma would beg to differ with that opinion. I have a picture from this time with Mamaw holding Mom. Professional pictures were few and far between, but she wanted to send a picture to my Grandpa, who at the time was stationed overseas. Mom was just a baby, barely two years old. All I could envision as Mom told me this story was the image of that baby girl standing up beside her beautiful Momma in that black-and-white picture. Eventually, my Grandpa came home from being stationed abroad. One night he was going into town and decided he would take Mom along with him for the attention it would bring. On the way into town, they ran out of gas on the dark backroads. My Grandpa left my Mom, at two years old, in the car while he walked over a mile into town for gas. It was getting late, it was dark, and so my two-year-old Mom laid down in the seat of the car and went to sleep. I imagine she was scared, lonely, and probably even cried. When my Grandpa returned, the doors to the car were locked. He became furious, banging on the windows and car doors in a drunken fury, trying to wake my Mom up. I am not sure how long it took him to get her awake and alert enough to unlock the doors, but by the time she was awake, he was in a fit of rage that could not be stifled. Mom's voice still shakes to this day when she tells how severely he beat her. When they finally returned home, she was still sniffling and despondent, and she remained that way for many hours. This is the part of the story when I asked my Mom where the car keys were during this ordeal. The keys were in his coat pocket the entire time. I cannot understand the illogical reasoning behind this. My heart still aches every time I recall my Mom sharing this story with me.

When my son was two years old, we lived in a 3rd story apartment in Moody, Alabama. We had a small storage room on the balcony. One evening I had opened the sliding glass door to place something into the storage closet and before I knew what had happened Eli had closed the door, and you guessed – locked it. I begged him for 30 minutes to unlock the door, but being two years old he could not understand, much less realize the predicament he had placed me in. As I watched him lay down on the carpet in front of me and watch Blue's Clues, I began debating whether I felt I could safely shimmy down the outside of the balconies from that high without falling. It did not seem likely and my heart was racing. I knew I was probably going to have to get someone to call the fire department to come and save the damsel in distress because it was after hours and the property office was closed. It seemed like an eternity had passed before someone came by that I could get to acknowledge me and help. Before calling 911 they decided to check the office although the lights were out and it was after hours. After much persistence, and much to our surprise, someone finally opened the door. They had been working late to get caught up on paperwork. After over an hour on that balcony I was finally back in my apartment with my little renegade. There was a lesson learned that night for sure. Not once did I scold him. Not once did I lay a hand on him. He was a baby and it was me, the adult, who did not use good judgment. To this day I will never understand why my Grandpa did the things he did, nor will I fully understand the life my Mom had to endure.

 My Mamaw had been taken out of school at the age of 12 to help raise her 14 siblings. Her lack of education kept her trapped in a perpetuating cycle she seemed helpless and hopeless to change. My Mom has lived in more states than she cares to recall.

She tells stories of her life, all of which are dotted and marred with memories of lack, poverty, abuse, rejection, and wrought with hardship. She has a few good memories from childhood, but most have been overshadowed by the impact of depression. She never had long-term stability or friends growing up until she reached high school. The lasting effects and far reach of the poverty my Mom experienced have been crippling for her. Despite how far she has come, to this day she deals with the lasting imprint and influences her upbringing had in her life. These are impressions that get embedded into DNA and passed down genetically through the generations. These generational curses must be broken to obtain freedom for ourselves and future generations to come. If we choose to ignore them, believing we alone are strong enough to overcome them, more than likely they will just show up in a generation or two down the road again.

When I was in fourth grade my mom went to work full-time. With Mom working and money not nearly as tight as it had been, more unsupervised consumption of junk food became more frequent than in the years before. These highly processed and specifically engineered foods designed to addict us from an early age were performing perfectly according to their design. Because we had grown up without daily access to junk food, I found myself very quick to over-indulge. (Remember that self-fulfilling prophesy I spoke about earlier?) I have an addictive personality and nature. I believe this is a trait that was passed down genetically from my Grandpa who was addicted to alcohol. My drug of choice became food. I enjoyed it. All of it. I found that it did not reject me. It comforted me. The summer before I started fourth grade we had moved from the boonies of Shelby (which I loved) to the big city of Columbiana. Well, it seemed that way although Columbiana is a perfect picturesque postcard of a small-town Hallmark movie. One afternoon as I begged for another popsicle, my Dad gruffly and sternly shouted, *"No, you're getting to be as big as the side of a house."* My Dad did not mean to hurt me. He was never a man of many words. He often did not understand his own emotions, much less how to express himself to others in ways that would not be harmful. That day I remember running and hiding in my closet, crying my heart out in pain. I had little concept of a healthy relationship with food, or the original design and purpose of food. I could not understand why my Dad yelled such hurtful words at me. I wanted to disappear and never be found. I was crushed. Once again, I unknowingly reinforced my previous declaration that when I grew up no one would tell me what I could and could not eat.

My Dad grew up in a harsh environment as well. His parents had divorced when he was young.

Daddy Louie, although kind and humble, was a hustler and a sneakster. He was a thief. He could not be trusted any further than most could pick him up and throw him. I remember meeting him a few times when I was young, but by that time he was already very elderly and in extremely poor health – completely bedridden. Mom tells the story of one Christmas when Daddy Louie gave us all gifts that had been stolen from his place of employment. When Mom found out the gifts were stolen, she packed everything up and had my Dad take it down to the local sheriff's office, who didn't know what to do with it. She did not want to have anything to do with the stolen items, nor did she want any of it in her home. My Dad's Mom, Little Mama, loved her family, but she ran a tight ship where it was her way or the highway. She was harsh, strict, and often lacked in expressing gentleness. Children were to be seen and not heard, and rarely allowed to have expressed emotions or opinions. This way of life was a result of her upbringing, passed down to another generation. As I dug deeper to learn more about my lineage, I discovered that as a child she was often ridiculed, she was often looked over, reared in absolute totalitarianism, and lived in an environment that also lacked grace.

Our pastor has always said, *"Show me your friends and I'll show you your future."* When my Dad was 12 years old, he found himself in the wrong place at the wrong time. As loving as she was, punishment never fit the crime when it came to the parenting methods of my Little Mama. Regardless of the offense, the reaction and responses Daddy and his siblings received were typically overly harsh and unjust. Every infraction was a mountain to die on. When my Dad realized what his friends were up to that fateful night, vandalizing some vending machines, he wanted no part of it. However, he found himself trapped and without an escape or way home. Despite the other young men testifying that my Dad had not participated in the crime, nothing was done to seek justice on his behalf. The other families had hired legal representation for their sons, and as a result they all served minimal consequences. This would not be the case for my Dad - the hammer came down on him. He was sent to a boy's home in Birmingham for two years, during which time he was not allowed to see his family. He was 12 years old and simply in the wrong place at the wrong time. It was during this time he would begin to allow a wall to be constructed around his young and tender heart, a wall that inadvertently hardened his heart towards God and towards his Mom. This is a story many in our family know nothing of because it was never spoken of. It was difficult for my Dad to share with us, and I am grateful for his bravery. This season in his life had an immensely negative impact on his self-worth and psyche. This experience broke my Dad's spirit and how he viewed justice in the world. He became angry as a young teenage boy. He would fight hard for the rest of his life to undo the impact of that one season of life when he was 12 to 14 years old. That wall he erected around his heart would also inhibit his ability to allow trust and love to penetrate through. Daddy was known as a tough guy growing up, but it was all an act to prove he was in control of his destiny, and not anyone else. Out of this season more strongholds and generational bondages were birthed.

As a result of this ordeal, Dad developed a very fractured relationship with his Mother. This relationship would not be repaired until years later when my Momma stepped on the scene and implemented those Sunday lunches I spoke of earlier. My sweet Momma was insistent on my Dad repairing his relationship with his Momma, forgiving and living peaceably with her. That is a story most in our family are not aware of, so I am telling it - because it needs to be told!

My earliest memory is that of riding my Big Wheel in the front yard of the small house where we lived in Shelby, Alabama. The small town of Shelby had an elementary school, as well as a few churches, and two competing gas stations. Mind you, these were the only two stores in town when I was little, except for Pate's Bait Shop of course. I cannot recall the name of the one we lived directly behind because it was the other gas station, B&B, that we frequented. I loved B&B because they always had hand-scooped ice cream cones. Ice cream was an uncommon delicacy in those days. Occasionally Mom and Dad would surprise us with an ice cream cone on the way home from church. It would take an eternity for me to decide which flavor I wanted. Let me just tell you - those were the days we lived for and looked forward to. Those ice cream cones might as well have been bags of gold to my brother and me. What we didn't understand at the time was Dad was giving up his drink money for the work week (he would buy a soda each day to have with his packed lunch) so we could have those ice cream cones.

 I could not have been more than three years old on that summer day, possibly two, but I remember the moment vividly. I was wearing my orange one-piece shortalls. Pretending I was going to the grocery store (of course – food), I carefully navigated my Big Wheel across the yard (my highway), making a right turn down alongside the fence, being certain to signal for any oncoming traffic of course. If you are not privileged enough to know what a Big Wheel is, let me go ahead and say right here and right now - I am genuinely sorry you have missed out on one of life's truest forms of joy for kiddos in the 1970s. A Big Wheel was a low-riding tricycle with two small wheels in the back with one large wheel in the front. The Big Wheel was highly popular and anybody who was anyone had one. And WE HAD ONE, therefore we were SOMETHING and SOMEBODY!

As I drove ever so carefully down this highway of mine, I continued down alongside a fence that was on the side of our front yard. The next thing I remember is extreme and excruciating pain like needles puncturing my entire body. I begin to let out blood-curdling screams, the kind of screams where parents immediately know that danger is lurking and something is terribly wrong. My parents came rushing out of the front door to find my entire little body swarmed with yellow jackets. I had disturbed a nest that had been built in the ground with my Big Wheel. They begin stripping my clothes off and knocking the yellow jackets off me, getting stung themselves as they were pulling them out of my hair. Yellow jackets are very aggressive and their delivery of a venomous sting is extremely painful. They can sting multiple times, unlike honeybees who leave their stingers in their victims. The pheromones released when they sting signal for them to sting their victims more. The more the victim reacts and slaps, instead of remaining calm, the more they sting; as if anyone could remain calm when being swarmed by yellow jackets, especially a small child.

My Little Mama was there and had gone to grab a container of snuff. Little old ladies with cans of snuff in rural Alabama in the late 1970s was not an uncommon occurrence. It was widely accepted and used as a remedy by many of the old-timers. To be honest, it still is to this day. It is believed to reduce inflammation caused by the venom in the stings, thus reducing the pain. As to whether this practice will ever be recognized by the medical community is still yet to be determined – however, it should be recognized in my opinion. Within minutes of my tiny body being wet and rubbed down with snuff I began to calm down. My parents wrapped me in an old orange bath towel that was frayed on the edges and made a bee-line (no pun intended) for the clinic in town. The doctors and nurses thought I was in shock because I was no longer crying from the horrible incident. They even snickered when they unwrapped me to see my body drenched in snuff. To this day I believe that one quick action by my parents and Little Mama made all the difference in how my body reacted to this traumatic experience. In the days that followed, I have flashes of memories of taking oatmeal baths in an old green bathtub. This memory is a reminder that in life everything can change in an instant and without any warning. The quick actions and response times of others around me more than likely were what saved me that day.

The American Psychological Association defines trauma as an emotional response to a terrible event. Integratedlistening.com defines it this way, "Trauma is the response to a deeply distressing or disturbing event that overwhelms an individual's ability to cope, causes feelings of helplessness, diminishes their sense of self and their ability to feel a full range of emotions and experiences." What happened to me that day was the traumatic event, but not the trauma itself. Trauma was the after-effect and impact of the event that occurred as a result.

I believe the reason that memory is so vivid in my mind nearly 46 years later is because it was incredibly distressing. Even as a young child, I remember the feeling of complete helplessness, although I could not have used that term at the time. Trauma crosses all lines of race, gender, ethnic and social backgrounds, and financial classes. Trauma is not picky and does not discriminate. It peers into every circle, invites itself into every culture and society, crosses every time zone, and permeates every climate. Trauma is hard to define, in the sense that something traumatic to one person may not necessarily be traumatic to another. What is known about trauma is that lasting impressions are made at the time the traumatic event occurs. Unprocessed past traumas will resurface later in life because of these impressions in forms of emotional struggles, inability to maintain healthy relationships, as well as physical illness within the body. Trauma is generally triggered when an individual feels helpless to change their situation, when they feel they have been violated in some way, or they feel an overwhelming sense of fear over circumstances. Figuring out root causes (remember, I am a roots girl) will help us identify what is holding us back in life. Strongholds are born as a result because trauma often causes a person to become stuck. Those strongholds put down roots with the sole purpose of inflicting pain.

The traumatic experience of the Big Wheel yellow jacket attack left me with a healthy fear and appreciation of ALL flying insects. I can spot them from a mile away. I always keep multiple cans of wasp spray on hand and can empty a can in a nano-second if I feel threatened. I have covered the back porch more than once. Cracking the back door enough to slide my arm and can out, and peering through the blinds, I have unleashed an entire can on a single unexpecting flying insect. I have been known to freeze spiders and all creepy crawly things with a can of hairspray as well. Ants do not stand a chance because I will empty enough poison to control the ant populations of an entire country upon them. I cannot even stand to see them outside in their natural habitats. I want them nowhere around me. I remember my Dad used to pour gasoline on the big ant hills and set them on fire. Now, please hear me loud and clear – I am not promoting the use of, nor am I recommending, endorsing, or advocating for the incineration of innocent ants with cans of gasoline and fire. I believe it is DANGEROUS! However, this was an effective ant population control method he practiced regularly. At the time it was a relatively inexpensive approach as well. We grew up in the south and I am certain he grew up seeing his parents do the same thing.

The impact (the trauma) of this single traumatic event and experience leaked into other areas of my life causing anxiety and distress any time I felt overwhelmed or was placed into a situation I felt helpless to control or manipulate. There would be other traumatic experiences in my childhood, my adolescent years, and even my adulthood where the impact would continue to build upon previous events and would become the lens through which I viewed every situation of life. Strongholds were setting up residence in my life.

People deal with the impact of traumatic events in many ways – some healthy, and some not so healthy. My Dad developed a harsh exterior that oozed with an attitude of not caring due to his traumatic experiences; although nothing could have been further from the truth. For me, food was one of the ways I chose to deal with pain, uncertainty, lack, rejection, hopelessness, and fear. I chose food because food brought me comfort and joy. I remembered all those holiday events where my cousin and I spent countless hours eating and giggling over whatever it is young girls giggle about. I also enjoyed the preparation of the food. I could control food. I could manipulate food. Food did not pre-judge me and food could care less if I had the latest fashion fads or hairstyles. Food did not care if I had enough money to go to the salon several times a month for perfect nails and brows. Food could not express an opinion that did not match mine. Food did not say harsh words to me that damaged my spirit. I felt accomplished with my skills when it came to food and the preparation of wonderful and delicious meals and treats. My ability to learn new techniques in the kitchen allowed me to feel capable and able. I loved the attention that the food presentation afforded me as well. I loved the feeling that would overcome me when someone praised a dish I had prepared. This addictive nature began taking a turn when I began eating in secrecy and concealing my consumptions; an unfortunate route that would soon find me out. Food was numbing and provided an alleviation of pain, although it was always short-lived and would require regular hits to maintain its effectiveness. Food was also a genetic weakness and stronghold in my family line. This preset re-disposition to an inappropriate relationship and disordered eating pattern with food, coupled with my propensity to lean towards addictive patterns with a partiality to food, would lead to years in bondage with a slave driver called food. When all of this is married to a lack of knowledge about a proper human diet and proper foods to consume for satiety, a perfect storm develops and begins wreaking havoc. The book of Proverbs inclines us to seek knowledge and wisdom because without these nuggets people succumb to the influence of the condition of being uninformed. As an officer once told me when I was stopped for a traffic violation in my 20s, *"Ignorance of the law is no excuse missy."* There we have it. Truth. Our lack of understanding the truth does not make it any less prevalent and pervasive.

The Christmas family gatherings at my Little Mama and Daddy Cups' house from childhood are still etched in my mind to this day. Gifts were piled high around the enormous vintage (although not vintage at that time) TV cabinet which spanned across what seemed to be the entire wall. I am sure it did not, but my little mind at the time remembered it that way. Year after year we would gather, lining up in the living room to make our way through the tiny kitchen. The room to the right of the kitchen circled back around into the living room, making it a perfect flow of everyone herding through the kitchen. The counters and the table in the kitchen were packed with dish after dish of scrumptious foods that came only once, maybe twice a year. My cousin Kim was only one year older than me, so we grew up as the best of buddies. We would pile our plates high as we could with enormous helpings of food. Then we would make our way to the back bedroom off the side of the kitchen where we would sit and giggle for hours while eating. My cousin and I would make several unmonitored and unregulated trips back to the kitchen to continue our ongoing gorge fest. This was normal to us. Nothing about this seemed unusual or inappropriate. Holidays were about the food, not the family. We had no understanding that what we were doing to our bodies was causing long-term negative health consequences. To this day I do not know how we packed away so much food and did not get sick.

Ice cream, you scream, we all scream for ice cream. The box says a serving is a mere ½ cup. All I can say is whoever came up with that serving-size suggestion must not be a lover of ice cream and therefore clearly could never understand its siren call at 10:00 o'clock at night. Of course, they could not possibly be American either if they do not love ice cream, or at least a true Southerner. That is the only logical conclusion. Perhaps the ½ cup serving size is just a suggestion, right!? As teenagers we had the "one size bowl fits all" in our house. They were multi-purposed bowls. We used the same bowls for cereal, chili, soup, and you guessed it – ice cream! At best we would get three, maybe four bowls out of each carton. Yes, growing up ice cream came in one of those rectangular cardboard boxes. We would scoop large servings out with metal cooking utensils, and then top it off with chocolate syrup or any other goodies we could find hiding in the pantry. I remember Mom taking a pen and marking the level of the ice cream on the outside of the box. She threatened each of us within an inch of our lives if we touched it before she came home from work because she had not had her share yet. When we would stay the night with our Little Mama and Daddy Cups, we would always beg for them to make homemade vanilla ice cream. Little Mama's vanilla ice cream was the best and it was pure sugar. It contained several cans of sweetened condensed milk, several cans of evaporated milk, and several generous cups of granulated white sugar, vanilla, whole milk, and eggs. We would wait anxiously for the ice cream maker to work its magic. It was like Christmas bells ringing when the motor stopped churning. We would dip out serving bowl-sized portions and eat until our hearts were content, sometimes even going back for seconds.

It is common for parents to offer a special treat as a reward for good behavior to their children – mostly an unhealthy treat at that. When we were little, Mom would always promise us an ice cream cone or milkshake if we did not cry when we got a shot at the doctor. It broke her heart to see us cry. What parent enjoys seeing their child suffer – none! To avoid the pain of hearing us beg for deliverance, Mom would promise a trip to the local Dairy Queen if we could be tough. This taught us to stuff our feelings and emotions down, ignoring them, instead of learning to properly express our feelings and learn healthy coping skills to deal with our fears. In no way do I think my Mom did this intentionally. In fact, I know she didn't. I am certain she was trying to alleviate the pain and dread of the inevitable shot. I can still remember the anxiety of walking into Doctor Mitchell's office. I can still remember asking Mom if she thought we would need a shot. I can still recall tensing up and gritting my teeth, which made the shot hurt even more, bent on not showing any emotion so I could get an ice cream cone or milkshake. As innocent as this was on my Mom's behalf, it strengthened the growing belief in me that food was a reward and could numb pain.

I can also recall food being used as a form of punishment. Being sent to bed without dinner as a penalty for breaking rules that I did not understand and that had never been communicated seemed unfair and unjust. This rather ineffective form of punishment only served to teach me behavior modification. Unfortunately, behavior modification with an absence of a foundational understanding that brings a heart transformation will never have a lasting impact. It simply taught me to perform. I believe using moments like these as teaching moments to train up a child in the way they should go would have a far greater impact than punishment in the form of isolation and withholding of food. Whether food is being given as a reward or withheld as a form of punishment, the likelihood that an inappropriate relationship with food will be born is almost inevitable. Using something designed to uphold and sustain life as punishment, and withholding engagement and relational interaction in times when a child needs to feel acceptance and validation the most, breeds insecurity, frustration, and an incorrect definition of the true purpose of food. Establishing healthy eating habits can be challenging with children, thus using food to reward or punish only undermines the healthy infrastructure parents are trying to build. When we use food in restrictive patterns such as these, we begin to develop unhealthy coping mechanisms. Using food as a reward or as a form of punishment predestines many for a lifetime of struggles with regulating their consumption or withholding of food. It can lead to a lifetime of disordered eating and unhealthy food patterns.

In the South whenever there is a threat of snow or ice, everyone raids the grocery stores and buys

ALL the milk and bread. I do mean, ALL of it! I have never understood this. Milk and bread? Before my proper human diet revolution, I would have much preferred Oreo cookies, Little Debbie snack cakes, and Diet Dr. Peppers any day over milk and bread. Nowadays there are breads for every occasion, every diet fad, and every taste preference. There are farmhouse breads, sourdough breads, beer breads, light breads, multi-grain breads, whole wheat breads, honey wheat breads, 12-grain breads, high-fiber breads, low-carb breads, Italian breads, pretzel breads, brioche breads, cheese breads, French loaf breads, gluten-free breads, paleo breads, sugar-free breads, sweet breads – well, you get the picture. There are loaf breads, sliced and unsliced breads, bakery breads, hamburger buns, hot dog buns, hoagies, wraps, tortillas, pitas, rolls – well, once again, you get the picture. Growing up, however, there was only one type of bread besides biscuits and cornbread. The almighty loaf of Piggly Wiggly white sliced bread. If mom found it on sale for $0.69, or cheaper, then you would find several loaves tucked away in the freezer. It was our hamburger bun, our cinnamon toast, our garlic bread, our hotdog bun, and our sandwich bread. We generally ate through two, and sometimes three loaves per week. We used to love cutting off the crust and then squeezing the bread into a ball of dough before eating. Yes, it is possible I need bread therapy. I am a recovering bread addict. I could easily have eaten half a loaf in one sitting and did on many occasions.

A generational bondage or stronghold is an authority in the lineage of a family. It is a spiritual stronghold that has been passed down from generation to generation for a very long time, possibly even further back than one can trace. A generational bondage can rear its ugly head in a few different ways, yet maintain a single and primary characteristic. **These strongholds and bondages lie, set up pretensions, and devour all logic. They steal our ability to focus, seek to control our every thought, change our identity, and consume all our emotional energy. Their goal is to keep us distracted, disengaged, and inattentive.** As we begin to believe the lies more and more, the enemy becomes more audacious because he is feeling confident in his grip on our minds.

For example, in my family, there was a single generational bondage/curse of addictive behaviors. However, this single curse showed up in many forms. Through many generations it has emerged as alcohol addiction, food addiction, people pleasing and praise addiction, pornography addiction, sex addiction, and as substance and drug abuse addiction. It has chosen to manifest as addictions through consumption, excessive spending, and several other compulsive-driven behaviors. The singular primary bondage was addiction, although it manifested in numerous ways.

Another curse on our family was a spirit of poverty and lack. Generation after generation lived in poverty and scarcity, not only physically but also mentally and spiritually. This curse reached deep back into the lineage of my family. How far back I am still not sure. Although my brother and I never experienced the level of poverty our parents did, and although we never went without food or a roof over our heads, and although we always had warm clothes and shoes on our feet that fit us, we still lived without many of the luxuries that our friends had. We lived with a poverty mentality and scarcity mindset engrained into our DNA through a generational stronghold. It was part of our identity, an unfortunate heritage passed down to us from generations before. Despite the incredible sacrifices, hard work, and enormous efforts of our parents, the authority given to the enemy had not yet been revoked – no matter how much they worked.

My brother and I grew up knowing a single hiccup could completely disrupt and complicate our entire lives. This reality reigned over our heads for years as the unspoken gospel truth. As I grew into an adult, this was revealed and demonstrated in my life as a fear of waking up one day and not having what I needed to survive. Several difficult seasons Tom and I walked through in the early years of our marriage served as an underpinning for this belief system as well. I was terrified I would be cut off again and not have what I needed to survive. I truly believed I was only pretty and accepted if I had pretty clothes, trendy clothes, and awesome boots. I only felt safe if the entire house and all the freezers and pantries were stockpiled. I only felt secure, safe, protected, and safeguarded against all of the uncontrollable factors if I had made all the preparations to ensure my family's security in the wake of some sort of unforeseen event. My identity as a woman and all that encompassed was established and rooted in my ability to build a home that could withstand endangerment and threats from the outside world regarding our basic needs. I went so far as to purchase water purification tablets, siphoning tubes, exorbitant amounts of matches and lighters, kerosene, candles, and duct tape. Yes, DUCT TAPE, because that stuff will mend any broken thing! I would often buy in secret and rush home to hide all my purchases before my husband got in from work because I knew beyond any doubt he would not support this excessiveness. How could he support what he did not understand though? This was a spiritual issue. There was a massive root system I did not even understand at the time. The thing is - I knew my behavior was too much, yet I still felt compelled and driven. I did not feel safe, not yet. Too many times my security had been threatened because it was contingent upon the external factors. Too many times I had been left feeling helpless and hopeless. This fear coupled with the genetic stronghold was having a field day in my life.

Another identified generational curse upon our family has been one of mental illness and developmental disorders. Let me stop and preface everything I am about to share with this cover – **I believe that mental health struggles in all forms is absolutely and 100% real. I am not a doctor, nor am I a medical or health professional. I am simply someone who has lived the reality and impact, as well as experienced its far-reaching grips. I believe there are many root causes that contribute to these conditions. I also believe that medicine and therapy can be incredibly beneficial tools in helping those who are impacted live happier, more productive, and more joy-filled lives. A person's struggle with one of these mental health or neurological concerns does not affect their value or worth. For that reason, I implore you to seek professional assistance if you or a loved one is struggling.** With that said, I also believe many times entire family lines are cursed.

Mental illness and developmental delays has been woven into the very fibers of the tapestry of our family for as far back as I can remember and have been able to trace. I'm not certain how far back it reaches, nor of its origins. Our family has been marked for years by major depression, clinical depression, bipolar and manic depressive disorder, schizophrenia, sound sensitivity disorders, seasonal depression, panic and anxiety related disorders, anger management issues, multiple personality disorders, eating disorders, PTSD, behavioral complications, pedophilia, developmental delays, ADD, ADHD, unspecified mood disorders, oppositional defiant disorders, as well as Asperger's Syndrome and Autism Spectrum disorders – to name a few.

Psychological and behavioral disturbances disrupt lives and often disarm hope and purpose. Despite the varying degrees of severity, the impact is the same. Innocence has been stolen, perpetuating cycles have persevered, and the lies that proliferate have thrived and spread across multiple generations with mendacities that sound something like this:

This is just how it is. It has always been this way in our family and always will be.

All the males in our family are like this.

Members of our family are predisposed to these illnesses and diseases, and therefore there is nothing we can do but live with it and manage it.

We must accept it.

It is just the evidence and impact of the imperfect world we live in. It is because of sin and a broken world.

I recall my Mom mentioning one time that she had prayed and asked God that my brother would never have any biological children in hopes that it would break the generational line of mental illness. This may sound selfish and harsh, even unfair and unjust. I don't think it was, and my brother would tell you the same because of the life he has lived suffering with mental illness. As I think back on this, I realize that authority was never taken to enter into spiritual warfare against the strongholds and bondages that were holding my brother prisoner. My Mom was a praying woman of God. Many nights I would walk into the living room to find her on her knees in front of the recliner pouring her heart out to God. Prayers had been prayed for healing. Prayers had been prayed to break the bondage by not allowing the bloodline on the male side to continue. To my knowledge however, never had she prayed for the bondages and curses to be broken off our family through revoking the legal access and renouncing and repenting of that which gave the legal authority to begin with. What happened was it skipped right on to the next generation and became evident in my son and other family members instead.

Although we live in a world that collided with evil in the Garden of Eden, we do not have to bow to the ruler of this domain. We do have authority. We do have spiritual domain rights. As we learn to speak truth and life, we can change the narrative to reflect the nature of our Heavenly Father. When we remove the access given by binding the enemy and loosing the power of all of Heaven to rush in, we will begin to see notable changes in the atmosphere. We can take authority in the name of Jesus. We can renounce any involvement, repent, draw the blood line, and close the gap. We can render the enemy ineffective in our lives by taking back any legal access he was granted. We have a promise that God's word will never return void. It must fulfil its purpose. We have an assurance that God is not like man who lies, but God is God and by His very nature He cannot not lie. The native language of Satan is lies, not truth. God's native language is love, power, strength, peace, and soundness of mind. We can trust that anytime we have a negative dialogue playing out in our minds that it is from the father of lies himself. We have a powerful weapon in the word of God, which is portrayed as the sword of the spirit in the bible.

Finally, be strong in the Lord and in his mighty power. Put on the full armor of God, so that you can take your stand against the devil's schemes. For our struggle is not against flesh and blood, but against the rulers, against the authorities, against the powers of this dark world and against the spiritual forces of evil in the heavenly realms. Therefore, put on the full armor of God, so that when the day of evil comes, you may be able to stand your ground, and after you have done everything, to stand. Stand firm then, with the belt of truth buckled around your waist, with the breastplate of righteousness in place, and with your feet fitted with the readiness that comes from the gospel of peace. In addition to all this, take up the shield of faith, with which you can extinguish all the flaming arrows of the evil one. Take the helmet of salvation and the sword of the Spirit, which is the word of God. Ephesians 6: 10-17 NIV

In Ephesians 6, we read about the armor of God that we are to prepare ourselves with every day. Take notice that all our combat weapons are defensive, meaning they are designed to protect and shield us, except for one. The word of God, the sword of the spirit, is offensive. It is designed to assault the enemy. It storms the onslaught and renders the enemy defenseless and inoperable. Our job is to send the word. Speak the word. God's job is to perform the validity of the word; to fulfil its purpose.

You must come to a place where you declare – **ENOUGH IS ENOUGH!** You must recognize this for what it is – an ambush targeting you and your loved ones. There is a beautiful declaration of truth found in scripture that I love. We must come to place in our spirit where we hear the voice of God telling us that we have circled this mountain long enough. It is time to go a different direction. It is time for an about-face.

You have circled this mountain long enough. Now turn north, Deuteronomy 2:3 NASB

To turn is to simply go a different way. Movement does not always mean we are moving forward and making progress. How we turn and in which direction we turn is very important. Sometimes we can be constantly on the move, yet we are only moving in circles, much like a dog chasing its tail. Much like the children of Israel, we become exhausted, exasperated, and fatigued; too weary to fight any more battles and longing for anything that could offer us any indication or resemblance of hope and relief from the current struggle. The problem with this outlook is that it is deceptive. **It promises hope and delivers despair. It promises relief, yet delivers anxiety and apprehension. It promises liberation while delivering subjugation** – bringing its victims under the control and dominion of Satan.

It promises peace, yet delivers chaos. Despite its promising exterior, dream killing antics lie buried deep beneath the glistening façade. This is exactly where the enemy of our souls would have us pitch our tents, set up house, and live out our days. We miss out on our purpose when we are walking in circles yet never gaining ground. When we grow tired, we often succumb to what is easiest, yielding to the mentality *that "this is just the way things are."* We surrender to a slave mindset and slip into survival mode rather than thriving, prospering, flourishing, and living purpose driven lives according to God's truths.

The curses that have held me and my family as a prisoner of war in bondage and fear have been identified. These generational curses and bondages have held too many of us captive for far too long, enslaving our hearts to a faulty belief that we would never have enough, would never be enough, and would never amount to anything. Many times, throughout the history of mankind, prisoners of war have been captured, held against their wills in appalling and outrageous conditions, gravely mistreated and abused, and often slaughtered. Mental and emotional tactics were used to rob them of their dignity while weakening their ideology, self-esteem, and self-worth. They were often subjected to unreasonably hard labor by the enemy, all while being demoralized and dehumanized. The intent of the enemy was to break their spirit, rob their identity, and keep them from ever hoping in something bigger than their current circumstances. In isolation many were manipulated into believing they were invisible and disposable, not only to their fellow comrades and country, but also to God himself. This is the same approach Satan uses against God's children.

This is exactly how the enemy works through the establishment of generational curses and bondages in our lives. Somewhere in my ancestral line, a door was opened giving legal access into our family. **Once legal access was granted, evil began to do what evil does best – deceive, disarm, disappoint, dislocate, and deny.** These intergenerational strongholds kept me isolated in a faulty belief system for years, with a core conviction that I did not deserve anything better. It kept me locked in a prison that God never intended for me to be detained. As a spiritual prisoner of war, I felt vastly under armed to fight against the relentless advancements towards the health of my mind, my finances, my body and health, and my family. I was weak physically, mentally, emotionally, and spiritually. I was a mess. I felt helpless and hopeless. This is the sphere where Satan wants us to live.

BUT GOD. But God is saying – *Come up higher! You were made for more! I've got more for you! You were* *made for more than this! You can be free. Your family can be free. The price has been paid and victory already accomplished through the rescue mission of the Cross of Christ.*

Generational bondages and curses cause immense harm, danger, emotional pain, and discouragement. They seek to destroy, divide, and dominate. Their sole purpose is to administer suffering while paralyzing families and entire bloodlines in fear. Their goal is to prevent us from ever discovering purpose and making a difference. Their target is your soul, and their purpose is to prevent peace from standing guard. Because the devil recognizes and understands that he cannot keep an individual from saving grace, he focuses instead on preventing them from living a life of freedom. Daily we should be examining our hearts and asking God to show us open doors that need to be closed. These spiritual manipulations of Satan are manifested physically through an establishment of power in our lives that we find ourselves struggling to overcome.

We recognize that our families are under siege. We exalt the truth of God believing that deliverance and breakage of these curses, bondages, and strongholds are possible. We are not without hope. We cannot fight unknown battles with invisible enemies. We must recognize that we are at war. Spiritual warfare is very real. It is not pretend. We must acknowledge any part we had in our condition and repent. Sometimes we must look backwards and rediscover the why and the how in order to identify, nullify, and cancel out the contracts put against our lives, and the lives of those we love; the lives of those yet to be born into our lineage.

I have a natural bent towards being excessive. I like to say I am zealous, enthusiastic, and passionate about providing all my family needs, or may potentially need at some point, at any point really, in the future. This conviction is not inherently a bad thing, but it can lead to some very unbalanced habits if not monitored and kept in check. Now that I have awakened an awareness to and found freedom in this area, God and I have set healthy boundaries that allow for me to keep a generous three-month supply of food, toiletries, cleaning products, emergency supplies, and the like in our home. I think being prepared is scriptural and no different than having a savings account or preparing ahead for retirement. However, a disproportionate and lop-sided way of viewing life can lead to an uneven rutted out ravine where we can become stuck. If we are not careful, our passions can become idols that we venerate more than God, all in the name of being a biblical and wise "Proverbs 31 Woman." Oxford Languages online dictionary defines excessive as "more than what is necessary or normal." It is an uncontrolled and unregulated behavioral pattern that is unrestricted and generally unreasonable when it comes to logic and trust.

I would love to know who came up with the idea that six ounces was considered a concrete and reasonable measurement for coffee. For me, six ounces is barely enough to make my eyeballs wake up and slap my body parts into action each morning. Instead of a serving of coffee in a standard size coffee cup, I want my jumbo mug that holds 18 oz. Okay, it holds 20 oz., but who is counting! I love that mug. It is my favorite Pioneer Woman coffee mug. The colors are beautiful, warm, and inviting, not to mention that it fits in the palm of my hand perfectly. There is nothing worse than a mug that does not comfortably fit into the palm of your hand with ample spacing for your fingers to fit through the opening of the handle. My husband recently discovered this truth when he found his favorite mug. It was a hand-crafted clay mug he found in the Smokies. He loved it so much he bought a second one on another trip we took a few months later.

One day I accidently knocked my favorite mug off the kitchen counter. My heart sank as the mug shattered into dozens of little fragments. I was devastated – devastated over a coffee mug y'all. I am talking bring out the handkerchief, and cry me a handful type of devastation. It was a discontinued style and pattern, and the likelihood of my finding another would be slim to none I was certain. My only hope was to find one hiding out in a thrift shop one day. I surrendered to the obvious that my beloved mug was gone and tried to press on. Several weeks later a little box showed up at the house. When I opened it, I was overwhelmed with joy and excitement to see my favorite coffee mug. My husband had searched and searched online until he found one exactly like the one I had broken on eBay. He says it was the most expensive coffee mug he had ever bought. That coffee mug is a true treasure to my heart and a reminder of my sweet husband's love. I could never put a price tag on this special gift.

Our guest bathroom is my storage for extra toiletries and medications. The cabinet underneath the sink is stockpiled with extra shampoos, conditioners, lotions, and deodorants, not to mention a basket of dozens of tiny little bottles of travel-size products I snatch from the hotel rooms before leaving. I completely ignore the fact that we never, ever use these tiny little bottles. My theory is two-fold. We may in fact need them one day and we have already paid for them in the cost of the room, so why not?! Do an about turn and open the closet door in our guest bathroom and you will find the true treasure trove of goodies. At any given time, you will find 20+ rolls of paper towels, 50+ rolls of toilet paper, extra gallons of water in case the world unravels at the hem, first aid products, medications, vitamins, and at least a 6+ month supply of different toothpaste products, toothbrushes, mouthwashes, and the like. We will not talk about the time I ordered 80 rolls of toilet paper from Amazon during the great toilet paper shortages of 2020. The fear was real guys. You will also find an ample supply of Covid19 home test, latex gloves, paper face mask, and hand sanitizer in this closet – none of which I use on a regular basis.

We have an ample storage of ground coffee (which I love), dried beans and rice (which I never eat), oats and dehydrated potatoes (which I never eat), and dried pasta (which I also never eat) for long term food storage should mass destruction change our way of living. I am not a doomsday prepper by any means, and I am not saying there is anything fundamentally wrong with prepping, but I have found that I feel safe and secure with a stocked house. I also feel more accomplished with a stocked house. I make our general cleaner for counters and floors, but the cleaners I still purchase are several deep on the laundry room shelves. I never buy one can of hornet spray, I always by the two or three pack. One box of trash bags is never enough, I want two boxes, and of course – all the different sizes too. Although we never cook with charcoal, I feel safer having three bags sitting on the back porch just in case they are needed. I save lint from the dryer and empty toilet paper rolls as fire starters, although we never start fires with them. Never. If I am buying seed packets to plant, one packet is never enough. I want to buy two or three packs. You will also find at any given time (most of the time) at least three or four bottles of laundry detergent and two massive bottles of dishwashing liquid on hand.

As mentioned before, being prepared for life is considered wise and we should be diligent to make sure our family's basic needs are met should the unthinkable occur. If 2020 and 2021 taught us anything, it should have been this simple and powerful nugget. Where the line is crossed is in becoming fearful. God has not given us a spirit of fear. As God's children we have access to an inheritance of love, power, and a sound mind. That means that we do not operate as the world operates. We do not buy into panic and hoarding. We do not buy into anxiety. We put our trust in the one who is the very epitome of trustworthiness. God does not just give us hope, rather He is hope. God does not just give us peace, rather He alone is the very essence of peace. God does not just strengthen us for the battle, He is the embodiment of strength. God does not just deposit love within us – God is love. We are made in His likeness to reflect His very nature. Because of this we can remain calm when everything around us is falling apart at the seams. Because of this we can maneuver with a spirit of wisdom and discernment. In Genesis 50:21 we are assured through the kindness of our Father that we do not have to fear because He will provide and take care of us and our families. We are to do our due diligence, doing what we can and should do, all the while trusting God to do that which only, He can do. Our action moves Him to act on our behalf. When we establish and root ourselves in Him, He will establish us according to His plan and perfect will.

Satan's greatest fear is authentic Christians who understand that spiritual warfare is real. Satan must bow at the name of Jesus. Satan cannot trespass against the bloodline of Jesus. The word of God cannot return void when it is sent out. In John 8, Jesus used the word of God to combat the attempts of Satan to deceive him, distract him, and disarm him. When we know who we are, and whose we are, then we will realize the One living inside of us is far greater than what is staring us in the face. As we live a life that is surrendered to the Lordship of Christ, we can be certain that those with us are far greater than those we see in the natural. Weapons may form, but they will not prosper. Waves may seek to crash down upon us and take us under, but we are hidden in the safety of the cleft of the rock.

CHAPTER 13
A CLEAN SLATE

Rooted in the love of God, the deepest recesses of our hearts are cared for so complexly that our spiritual appetite is intensified and increased to contain the extravagant love He pours out upon us. He lavishes us with this great love through many facets and channels, all intricately connected and weaved together into a beautiful tapestry displaying His iridescent, kaleidoscopic splendor. Without His inpouring we would be incapable to contain all He has for us. It is in His great love for His children that He equips us to be who we were designed and created to be. Without Him we are mediocre at our best, and unknown and insignificant at our worst.

How many of you remember the old chalkboards in school? I think for the most part nowadays dry erase and wet erase boards are the norm, as well as computers and digital touch screens, of course. Back in the day however, my day, a chalkboard was the hallmark of the classroom. They seemed to stretch across an entire wall for the whole length of the classroom. I remember one of my elementary school teachers seemed to have it out for me from the beginning. She simply did not like me or my Mom – at all. It was evident. I wish I were overreacting, overdramatizing, and over assessing this memory from my childhood, but I am not. In fact, her dislike of me was so obvious and apparent that my Mom had to get involved on multiple occasions. You can imagine my dismay when we discovered this 2nd grade elementary school teacher would also be my 4th grade elementary school teacher as well. The struggle was real y'all. Granted, I loved to talk - I couldn't help it - and as a result I often found my name on the right side of the chalkboard located on the center wall of the trailer of my 2nd grade classroom. I often found myself writing sentences on this chalkboard as a form of punitive punishment for not keeping in line with my teacher's rules. In all honestly, although I was a child and acted as such, I was never going to be able to gain her stamp of approval. Sometimes my name would end up on the chalkboard for no reason at all, just simply because I never seemed to be able to earn her acceptance and endorsement. I was often used as her goat, and that does not stand for *GREATEST OF ALL TIMES*, to teach all the other students a lesson on "what not to do," or "how not to act." I recall one occasion when she was scolding several students who had been playing in the bathroom where in her reprimand she declared, *"now Jennifer, I expected this behavior from Valerie, but not from you."* On another occasion I was complimenting my teacher on how pretty her coloring was on the bulletin board, to which she replied, *"Yours could be too if you would just try and put forth some effort."* Another nail was hammered into the coffin of rejection.

Her disapproval and continual condemnation of me as a little girl left a mark that honestly, I remember to this day. My name on the chalkboard meant that when we went outside for recess, I would have to sit on the ground with my legs crossed for 5-10 minutes - or whenever my teacher had decided I had paid my penance - before I could join in swinging from the monkey bars and climbing over the large tires that had been cut in half and made into playground equipment. Sometimes she would forget and I would sit there much longer before atonement had been made. My name on the chalkboard meant all my peers' eyes were on me as the one who could not follow the rules and be a team player. My name on the chalkboard communicated that I was defective, unapproved of, unworthy, and not good enough. Once again, I was left feeling just short of acceptance. Often my name would be the only name on the chalkboard. My name on the classroom chalkboard, multiple times per week, communicated to my tender heart that I could never and would never measure up to the standards that everyone else seemed to effortlessly reach and uphold. Shame began to creep in and whisper to me that I was bad.

These memories are among some of my earliest experiences with rejections that left deep wounds in my heart. This was the beginning of my people-pleasing behaviors that would follow me well into adulthood. There would be many times throughout my life that I would find my name on the chalkboard of life and in need of a clean slate, a do-over, a fresh start. As a young child, I can recall feeling a sense of relief when I would arrive at school the next day to see my name erased and a clean slate to start the new day. For my name to be erased, someone had to physically take an eraser and wipe my name from the board. This is what Christ did to give us all a clean slate. He physically came and gave His life to wipe our sins away and to give us a clean slate with God. A clean slate is a breath of fresh air; a warm and inviting aroma. It is a deep exhale of tension and anxiety, of stress and heartache, with an even deeper inhale of God's incredible grace.

We live smack dab in the center of God's beautiful and picturesque masterpiece of sunrises and sunsets. The morning skies are often orange and pink, almost seeming to be ablaze with waves of fire. The evening skies are like taking a deep breath and realizing that this is our home and that we get to view this stunning and exquisite display of artistry. It is a composition of God's heart every single morning and evening. A clean slate is like this morning sun shining brightly as it dawns a brand-new day. It is like this evening glow of the stars that light the dark sky and kiss the world goodnight. A clean slate is a new lease on life, a fresh bounce in your step, and a deep sense of longing that has been filled. It is a refined fire burning deep within, and a renewed sense of hope that breaks each new day. It is the rainbow signifying a promise. It is a good, hard belly-laugh – medicine to the soul you know; a deep joy brimming and bursting forth in an overflow of gratitude and love. A clean slate is a sigh of relief that we will never have to live every waking and sleeping moment of our lives in a prison of fear and ridicule ever again. This is God's design; His story of redemption. His story of restoration. His story of healing. The striking and prominent emphasis here is, "HIS!" Once again, nothing about this story is essentially about me. I am just a character in the story. It is all about Him! His arresting love that chased me down and would not let me go. His desire is for me to live a life filled with confidence, running after, and pursuing Him through fulfillment of purpose and destiny; a purpose and destiny laid out long before the foundations of this world were ever formed.

The online Free Dictionary by Farlex defines "clean slate" as an opportunity to start over without prejudice. A clean slate is a fresh start without bias, without judgement, without any partiality, without predisposition, without discrimination, and without preconception. Who would not want that? New beginnings are an extravagant gift from God lavished upon His children. A clean slate gives us the opportunity to not only imagine our lives living in the fullness of all our God created us to be, but also in the opportunity to possess it!

What would the best version of yourself look like? Have you ever given much thought to this potentially life-altering question? What are your hopes, dreams, and desires? What would you change or keep the same? Where would you go and what would you do if there were no limitations? Who would you befriend, or who would you leave behind? What inspires you to go the extra mile? What doors would you close forever, and which new doors would you be courageous enough to walk through? It will never be enough to just consider the possibilities my friend. We were created with enormous potential to do more than simply consider. We were created by God with gifts and talents, with purpose and destiny as unique as each one of us. So very few will ever rise above the circumstances and situations life has thrown their way to freely soar like eagles on the wings of determination; on wings of resolve and fortitude with a grit and strength that comes only from above. Do you have a resolve and tenacity to place a choke hold on your calling, to hold on tightly and not let go? The enemy will try to silence you and rip it from your hands. The enemy of our soul will stop at nothing to prevent us from ever recognizing our potential, our purpose, and will make silencing our megaphone of praise his ultimate goal. He will stop short of nothing to accomplish this because of his overall goal to silence love. It is about the bigger picture of stopping the Kingdom of Heaven from coming to kiss earth.

Faith is not works-based, but our faith should drive us to do the works God designed for us to do long before we were ever a thought in our parent's minds.

For we are God's masterpiece. He has created us anew in Christ Jesus, so we can do the good things he planned for us long ago. Ephesians 2:10 NLT

We are meant to be an active reflection of our Father. We are created in His image and likeness. We were never meant to be spectators or observers. Shame, guilt, fear, insecurity, and the temporal will try to paralyze us into sitting in the audience as an onlooker instead of participating as an essential and important member of the body of Christ. The shame that comes from our names being on the chalkboard of life are meant to disgrace, dishonor, embarrass, humiliate, and silence us. So often in life, even when we are given a new opportunity to have a fresh start, our past is still held over our heads to make sure we don't color outside the lines. Behavior modification has never done anything more than contribute to hardship by addressing external conduct and outward components instead of internal causes and roots.

If we are going to live in freedom, we must get to the heart of the matter and experience a heart revolution and transformation. When shame is placed upon us like a garment of clothing, we fail to realize our worth and value; our potential. My teacher never spoke kindly to me. She always thought the worst and held the previous days failures to comply with her rules over my head. Her constant ridicule succeeded in causing great shame to enter into my life. Mid-way through the school year, I felt as if everyone else in my 2nd grade class was better than me. We find all through Scripture many examples of training and living disciplined lives – habits and disciplines that produce healthy and vibrant individuals. Punishment demands the sacrifice of an individual's dignity and respect. Jesus trained his disciples, gently giving a rod of correction through examples of disciplined living and disciplinary actions. He did not demoralize them and deflate their personalities and spirits. He did not depress them. He did not yell at them. He never used them as a direct example to others of how not to live. There is a huge difference in these two approaches. Heart transformation can only be born out of love and investment into relationships. Heart transformations are the result of tenderness and teaching that does not demand its own way.

The focus is on the person and developing them, rather than shaming and demanding that one fall into line with specific pre-formed patterns.

I know this all too well in my life. Satan has tried to silence me through fear tactics, intimidations, words meant to destroy me, addictions, abuse, and mockery of my dreams. I have been told I would have to settle for whoever would have me. I have been told I was not anointed only moments before going onto stage to lead praise and worship. I have been told I should sit down and remain silent by the leader of a "prayer group" in our church I attended at the time. I have been told I was not good enough and I have been told I was too much. I have been abused and I have abused myself. My life has been endangered and threatened. My desire and inclinations to write as a young teenage girl were extinguished by a "concerned" family member, instead of encouraged and cultivated. I have been made to feel invisible, disposable, unwanted, undesirable, unappreciated, unloved, unapproved, misunderstood, and rejected. Truth (when fully known and applied) always trumps and triumphs over the propaganda and mal-intent of the enemy. Read that again!

Truth Always Triumphs! **Truth applied will surpass every lie designed to purposely bring harm to us and take us out. Truth outperforms and** exceeds even the wildest of dreams. Truth can never be silenced. Truth is fact. Truth is certain. Truth is the only real reality and collides with man's definition of reality. Truth is actual. Truth is exact. Truth cannot be disputed.

The truth is I am accepted by Christ. His opinion of me is the only opinion that matters and stands. I am a new creation in Christ. I am made anew, afresh, over, and without spot or blemish because of the Blood of Christ. I have a clean slate. This clean slate does not hold past setbacks in suspicion over my head. There is no need to continue the resurrection of the old man when God says He is ready to do a new thing. I do not have to wear the garment of shame. In Christ Jesus I have wisdom, I am righteous, sanctified, healed, healthy, whole, restored, and redeemed. Even though I am inadequate in every sense of the word on my own, I also know what God's promises say about who I am. You see, when God sees me, He sees me through the lens of the Blood of Christ. I am loved beyond measure. The hardening of my mind is gone and I have the mind of Christ. I am presented before my Father as clean. I am justified. I am valuable. I am transformed. I am accepted. I no longer resemble the person I used to be. I am represented by Christ and I reflect my Father. My Father is not disappointed in me. I am called. I am intelligent. I have something to bring to the table. I am creative. I am not mediocre. I can do all things through Christ who enables me and equips me. I am chosen – so, Why not ME? Why not YOU?

We are beautiful. We are the apple of our Father's eye. We are blessed. We are above and not beneath. We are the elect. We are sons and daughters of a King – THE KING! We are His favorite! We fight from victory, not for it. We are fearfully and wonderfully made. We are NOT who others say we are. We are set free, confident, strong, and never forgotten - never alone. We are men and women after the heart of God. We are generous and kind. We are included in God's circle. We are called the friend of God. We are accepted, rescued, restored, and we are enough because Christ is more than enough! We are all uniquely gifted and talented to do what God set in place for us to accomplish. We can do all things through Christ Jesus because His strength is made perfect in our weakness. As children of God, we are blessed in our coming and in our going – because Christ has taught us how to enter in and how to exit. We are highly favored by God and man. God blesses the work of our hands because we submit all we do unto Him to be filtered through His plan and will. The work of our hands aligns with His heart. We are born of the Spirit and we are citizens of Heaven, forgiven, and grafted into the vine.

I have come to realize that the way my teacher treated me for two school years during my elementary education spoke mostly about her own insecurities and brokenness. I also recognize she is a child of God in need of healing and rescue. She is a child created by God and He loves her very much. For this reason, I freed her long ago from the impact she made on my fragile child heart. I remember all she did, but all she did no longer has a choke-hold on my life. I am not crippled by what the enemy tried to accomplish through her. God took what was meant for evil and used it for my good. We flipped the script and now we use it to point others to Jesus.

Satan does not want us to realize that we can have a clean slate through Christ Jesus. He wants us to remain stuck in the pit of despair, mistakes, discouragement, fear, worry, anxiety, depression, dejection, and rejection to name a few. What pit are you stuck in my friend? Do you know that we are called to be resolute? Satan will try to extinguish deep joy in our lives that leads to ultimate freedom; the abundant life God has called us to and always longed for us to live in. May we never forget Jesus died for this life we are living. May we steward our lives well. Our lives are valuable and they are a treasure. Are we living in a way worthy of His death and His resurrection?

Have you ever been handed the opportunity to give someone in your life, whether in close relationship or by association, a clean slate? Perhaps, like me, there have been times you needed to extend this gift when you did not feel like it. The thing about feelings is they are unreliable, unpredictable, and a faulty basis on which to establish decisions. Feelings keep us preoccupied and fascinated with crazed obsessions and sentiments that shape our attitudes towards others. Unfortunately, these attitudes are often skewed. As humans, we have mastered the art of categorizing sin and wrong doing because we deem certain immoralities or offences to be less vilifying and slanderous than others. Often, we - me included - overlook our own disgraces while at the same time shredding to pieces the infringements and violations of others. While it is true that the Bible speaks of sins and sins unto death, meaning sins for which atonement can be made and sins for which we choose to carry ourselves, we find the answer to this uncertainty undeniably clear in the book of Revelation.

The one who conquers will have this heritage, and I will be his God and he will be my son. But as for the cowardly, the faithless, the detestable, as for murderers, the sexually immoral, sorcerers, idolaters, and all liars, their portion will be in the lake that burns with fire and sulfur, which is the second death. Revelation 21: 7-8 ESV

God does not hold the same viewpoint as we do. All sin requires atonement, whether that atonement be by the Blood of Jesus or by our own feeble attempts to carry and cover our sin, which is futile and in vain by the way. There are no good sins, lesser sins, and bad sins. There is no such thing as "little white lies." It matters very little if I agree with this or not. My assessment and my opinions are of no value in this matter. The Bible is very clear.

But your iniquities have made a separation between you and your God, and your sins have hidden his face from you so that he does not hear. Isaiah 59:2 ESV

For all have sinned and fall short of the glory of God, Romans 3:23 ESV

If we say we have no sin, we deceive ourselves, and the truth is not in us. If we confess our sins, he is faithful and just to forgive us our sins and to cleanse us from all unrighteousness. If we say we have not sinned, we make him a liar, and his word is not in us. 1 John 1:8-10 ESV

He is the propitiation for our sins, and not for ours only but also for the sins of the whole world. 1 John 2:2 ESV

The heart is deceitful above all things, and desperately sick; who can understand it? Jeremiah 17:9 ESV

I have heard it said that withholding forgiveness is much like drinking poison and expecting the other person to die. No one in their "right" mind would do such a thing. When we are in the deep pit of hurt however, we are not thinking clearly. We do not process clearly and certainly cannot trust our own advice. Withholding forgiveness is a protective and coping mechanism that tricks us into inexplicable behavior patterns that keep us in a bottomed-out quarry. My heart and feelings will deceive me and misguide me every single time I place my trust and hope in them instead of Jesus. The temporary fix I get from the dopamine rush my mind and body are receiving, oddly and incorrectly provides a short-lived comfort which deceives me. It will keep me in a perpetuating cycle of pain and heartache. It is like repeatedly pulling the scab off a wound. If I choose to not forgive and extend grace, then I am choosing to carry the weight of my own sin, because my sin cannot be compensated for. *(Please refer to our discussion previously on what forgiveness is and is not.)* I can never be enough to appease my own failures. Only the robust love of Christ can do that. It is only His forceful and full-bodied, intense, and rich love stretched out on a Cross that can provide atonement, not mine. I am not even close to being capable of accomplishing that.

As humans, we find it hard to grapple with the reality that sin, in all its many forms, is all wrong. While it is true that certain sins carry much heavier consequences than others, God still sees them all in need of atonement. There is pardonable sin that we allow Christ to atone, and there is sin in which we choose to carry ourselves because we refuse repentance and surrender. Still, it is sin that separates us from our Father. To be forgiven, we must forgive *(again, please refer to our previous discussion on what forgiveness is and is not)* – and that my friend also includes forgiving yourself. The offender's depravity is between them and God as to whether they will truly repent, surrender, and receive atonement, or choose to carry the weight of that sin unto death. Our choice, and we do get to choose, cannot be dependent upon another person's response to Biblical truth. We are responsible and accountable for our own personal response to truth only, not theirs.

A family member molested my brother and me, along with many of our cousins and some of their friends as well when we were little. Our parents knew nothing of this at the time. We were all silenced and paralyzed in fear and confusion. We told no one. The seeds of shame and guilt had been planted long before the truth would ever come to light and begin to be unraveled. This family member would spend five years on the run under an assumed name and stolen identity before finally being caught and spending 20 years in prison. Lives were destroyed, family relationships broken and severed, and innocence stolen. Many suffered greatly because of the actions of this one individual. It had been more than 25 years since I had seen this family member. Our untimely and undesired "family reunion" would occur at one of the most difficult times of my life – during the passing of my Dad. I despised his presence during this time of grief and mourning. I did not want him there. I did not want to talk with him. I did not want to see him. I didn't want to extend kindness to him. I could barely process these feelings consuming me during this difficult season of life, much less share them with anyone. Yet, I knew God had strategically placed him in our lives to provide help to my Mom during this season. My Mom was the care-giver for my 90-year-old Mamaw who was bed-ridden and living in my Mom's home. Contending with the mixed emotions of this revelation, layered with the pain of watching my Dad die, was insufferable and agonizing. Why would God bring this man back into our lives after more than 25 years, and at a time riddled with so much heartache? The hollowness of my soul was penetrating to the core. The emptiness frightened me. The lack of grace was alarming and upsetting. Yet, I still found it difficult to wrestle. It seemed almost cruel for God to expect me to extend grace and forgiveness when my heart was being shattered into a million tiny fragments as my Dad slowly slipped away. I was exhausted mentally, physically, emotionally, and spiritually. Those days seemed to be passing in slow motion while a vortex of chaos was consuming everything around me. Why would God require this of me? Why now? Why would God expect a sacrifice so great to be forged on the anvil of grace and love?

There will be times in your life when you will be required to rise higher. You will be required to extend forgiveness when you would rather do anything but. Often it will be at the most inopportune time when you feel the weight of the world pressing you into the ground, hammering you into the anvil of grace and love. The beauty of forgiveness is that when extended, you will discover you were the prisoner that was set free. You are the one who receives the do-over; the clean slate. Extending forgiveness lightens the load. It is a beautiful gift from our Father. You are the one given a fresh perspective and a new lens to view life. When I stopped trying to manipulate and control the situation and the outcomes, I was able to breathe and relax. It was only then I was able to find a resting place in God's bosom that enabled strength to rush in, equipping me to be what my Mom needed me to be. The ultimate test of our devotion to Christ is in our willingness to submit to His Lordship over our feelings, and even over our understanding. If I must understand what God is doing in my life before I will trust it and submit to it, then I am trying to control the situation – and that my friend is the opposite of complete surrender.

CHAPTER 14
THE POWER OF CONNECTIVITY

My life has been filled with many Red Sea Roads – many incredible opportunities for redemption and restoration, as well as divine revelations. To be completely and ruthlessly honest, an exorbitant amount of infamous *AHA* moments have been experienced by none other than yours truly. *AHA* moments in life possess the ability to bring along with them a hope alliance that grafts us into the beautiful tapestry of Christ. I am grateful for these revelations because they have exposed lies and given me the privilege of drawing closer to God and walking in joy and freedom that I could not have known otherwise. For this reason alone, I recognize their value and would never regret the trials and struggles they brought. I cannot recall a single struggle that in the moment was a welcomed, blissful, memory-making scrap book material experience; however, they were the most revealing and honest times of my life. These moments mandated deep authenticity, individuality, and originality because I am not a replica or copycat of another design. They required something of me that often I did not want to give. They stretched me and conditioned me. They challenged me and gave me wings to fly. They empowered me and dared me to be more than I ever thought or imagined I might be. They confronted the darkness within me, healed the broken spaces in my heart, and gave me courage to test the waters – wading out deeper and deeper with each step of faith. These moments have shaped and formed me into the woman I am today. For that alone I am grateful. I am grateful for a loving Father who sees fit to train and develop us, rather than keep us cowered in fear through punishment and shame. One of the most powerful revelations God has given me is this truth - there is immense power in connectivity and community. Keeping connected to the power source captivates our hearts and exhilarates our spirits. The strength found in being connected to one another and to God empowers us to take a daring stand against all odds. This strength and power stimulates and reinforces our core design, supports our spiritual skeletal system, and fortifies our mental, emotional, and spiritual retaining walls. Retaining walls prevent erosion and floods from destroying. They provide protection. Our connections with other humans are like retaining walls, helping to protect us from that which seeks to erode us spiritually, emotionally, and physically.

Being connected to others allows us to share the joys of life, as well as the sorrows of life, instead of bearing the weight alone. Being connected to a community equips us to fight a good fight. Staying connected provides protection from our spiritual blind spots as well. If there is one thing I know, I know that I do not give good advice when I am emotional. I am the last person on planet earth I need to be listening to when my vision has been jaded by whatever obstacle has been hurled at me, especially if I am exhausted and spiritually jaundiced. This was the case as we walked through the passing of my Dad. I give the advice of a two-year old when I have allowed myself to become burned-out, fed-up, or when I have been wronged, am in pain, or in a season of emotional stress. It is in the seasons of brokenness and grief, the seasons of weariness and loneliness, and the seasons of trial upon trial, that we need the support system that connectivity with God and others gives us. We were built for this connection. We were designed and wired to live within the protective layer of community. We will never fully thrive outside of this design, try as we may.

A few years ago, God blessed me with a new sweet friend which has since become very precious and dear to my heart. In fact, she was the first set of eyes on my first raw manuscript of this book, offering constructive criticism, edits, insight, and thoughts. I trust her completely and her opinion matters much to me. I had prayed for her. I prayed for her before I knew her. I needed a friend like her in my life. About eight and half years ago my two dearest friends walked away from me at the same time. I was devasted and crushed. I felt like a had a hole the size of a watermelon in my heart. I had made a choice they did not agree with and therefore they both decided that ending the relationship was the best option. Sometimes God is closing doors that need to be closed, and that closing will bring an initial sting and pain. We will not always understand the closing I walked through grief mourning the loss of these two friends who I had met in the first small group I ever joined at the church we attended. I could not have realized it then, but I can see clearly now in hindsight that God was leading me in a different direction. Remaining in those relationships would have taken me down an entirely different path that was not His perfect plan for me. God is always in the business of opening new doors when others are being closed. We must trust His timing and process. It was during this long wait that God began to condition my heart to **COMPLETELY** trust in and rely upon Him. He wanted to be my first resort, not my friends. He wanted His Holy Spirit to be my comforter, not my girlfriends. Walking this Red Sea Road helped me understand the delicate balance of community and connectivity. Even though we are designed to live in community with others, others can never become our number one. God must always be first.

    I went eight and a half years without a close sister friend in whom I felt I could confide until I met my Sunshine. I had several close friends that I knew I could call on and they would without a doubt be by my side in an instant if I needed them. I am grateful for these sisters in my life. I cannot imagine life without them. They bring light and laughter and joy – AND, we are truly stronger together. But - Sunshine is different. She is that soul-sister my heart longed for. She is the one whom I can process life with. She lives up to her name – a ray of light to all who know her. She just gets me. Everyone needs someone that just gets them, you know? Everyone needs that someone who understands them and never passes judgment on them. Everyone needs that special someone who laughs and cries with them, and who will even call them out when needed. We were designed to do life with those who will challenge, inspire, and encourage us; those who will be there in the cheering section of life, but also show up with the baseball bat ready to swing if need be. Sunshine has been such a gift to me. Even when life and all its responsibilities and demands keep us apart for weeks or months at a time, the soul connection we have stands firm. Our souls are starving for this sort of connection. It is by design we crave it - not a mistake. Connection brings a deep bond formed through being seen, being heard, and through knowing that we are not alone. When we feel understood and heard, we gain a sense of belonging. This belonging will require action and effort, however. It does not always come easy, but it is always worth it.

ALWAYS WORTH IT!

A baby in the womb is connected to its mother by the umbilical cord. The umbilical cord is the power source, giving life and nutrition that help the baby grow and develop. The same is true for the community we connect ourselves to in life. When we are connected by a spiritual umbilical cord to a life-giving community, we will grow and develop into the women of God that we were destined to become. When you are connected to something or someone, the natural and automatic outflow is lower levels of anxiety and depression, and higher levels of self-esteem. We have a greater sense of worth and value for both ourselves and others. Our ability to empathize increases through connectivity and belonging, as well as our ability to trust and build trust. As Hebrews 10:25 so eloquently explains, we are better together! We are stronger together. We are healthier together. I know it is hard to commit to living connected with others all the time, but I challenge you to be courageous and take the plunge. Let your guard down. We were built to need and depend upon one another.

If you ask an avid surfer which is better – surfing alone or with others – you are most likely to receive a myriad of answers. Most will say surfing alone trumps because they can enjoy the quiet tranquility of the experience, and the adrenaline rush, as well as make all judgment calls and choices on their own without distractions and interruptions. Surfing alone affords them to hold all decision-making power in their own hands, trusting their own insight and wisdom. However, most honest surfers would also agree that surfing alone is not always the wisest choice that could be made, despite its attractiveness and draw. Surfing alone can place a surfer in dangerous conditions without anyone else around to offer help, insight, wisdom, perspective from a different viewpoint, rescue if needed, or even encouragement and inspiration. Surfing alone also does not provide the surfer the benefit of a second pair of eyes that could spot that shark in their blind spot ready to make them a tasty morning snack.

We all have blind spots. Living in connection with others helps protect us from what we cannot see. What we do not see has the potential to take us under and out. Our blind spots can render us ineffective, inactive, and defeated on the battlefield of life. What we never see coming will paralyze us and derail our goals. Connection is the fuel that ignites the fire within us to do more and be more. When we are connected, life becomes about more than just us. Life becomes more about God. Life becomes more about others, and that my friend is what is at the heart of God - People. People are the heart of God. People were always the heart of the Cross; the very reason Christ came to Earth.

When I was around five years old, I found myself locked in a dark silent church one Sunday night - alone. Panic and fear set in and I lost every wit my five-year-old self had. In a dreadful attempt to find rescue, I began screaming and crying, banging on the doors. I can still see myself banging on those huge double doors that separated me from the darkness of the room and everyone I loved. As I described earlier in this book, I was a very timid child. I was almost always nervous around most people unless I knew them well. I preferred my aloneness over community even as a child, except for this night. My core design begged for connection. Something deep within me longed to be in community, and not locked inside a dark, cold church building alone. Thankfully I was not alone for too long and was reunited with my parents rather quickly.

Previously I shared that by late summer of 2018, my husband and I both were at a crossroads; each of us so deep in depression and angst that we couldn't see past our own hurt to see the condition of the other. I truly believe we were at a point of no return. As I look back, the most startling of all revelations was the lack of community and the lack of connection. There was no power source. We had no one to stand in the gap for us. No one to come along side us and help us. No one to challenge us in our actions and behaviors. Yes, we went to church. We served in church. We led small groups in church, yet we refused to allow ourselves to be vulnerable with these individuals God had placed in our lives. We always pretended to have a tight handle on life, always in control. We were good at doing the church thing, but we lacked integrity and even more sadly, we lacked any real and life-giving relationships to hold us accountable. There was no one to pull us out from the riptide currents of life when they came to sweep us under and out to sea. There was no one to love and support us, encourage us, and honestly – there never really had been. We were two very broken individuals who continued to break one another in an effort of self-preservation. Our focus on self-preservation made it impossible for us to be empathetic towards one another. We were doing our best to tread water and survive, pulling each other under in an attempt to stay afloat. The only defense mechanism we knew was shutting others out and running. The only coping mechanism we knew was substance abuse and addictions.

Connection and living in community will require action, interaction, vulnerability, and effort. I had grown up in church, but let me share a secret with you – **CHURCH ATTENDANCE DOES NOT AUTOMATICALLY EQUAL COMMUNITY OR SALVATION.** I was perfectly fine with doing life on my own, despite the wreckage and impact of doing things my way. This coupled with my natural bent of desiring solitude was the recipe for yet another perfect storm.

Today my husband and I run a local chapter of a national 501(c)(3) non-profit organization. We see the impact almost every single day of social poverty and isolation; the lack of healthy community and connections, or the impact of being connected to the wrong community. We witness first-hand the deception and lies of the enemy of our soul – the lie that we do not need others, that we are just fine on our own. This is the ultimate of all lies from the father of lies. Satan uses this lie to paralyze people or to keep them trapped in cycles. He does not want anyone to realize they were created for more than to simply exist and take up space. He uses this lie to deprive and cheat them of the authority and dominance they have access to in Christ.

Tommy and I know this darkness very well. Life-giving connections propel us into the promise and hope of God's truth. Connections empower us to live lives focused on the bigger picture of bringing Heaven to Earth. The lack of connection strips away our power and leaves us without a source to ignite this purpose and legacy. Lack of connection leaves us without a ladder to climb out of the pit. Sadly, this not only impacts us, but future generations and entire communities; the world at large. The overwhelming constant we see in the work we do is no family support, no life-giving connections, and no church family. So many are trying to keep their heads above the waters, but are becoming more exhausted, like Tommy and I were. The waves are carrying them further and further out. Their spirits are screaming on the inside, like my five-year old self locked in that dark church, desperately searching for someone to hear them; for someone to rescue them.

My Mamaw tells of a story on her small 1940s Alabama farm. She was about eight years old and her job was to collect the eggs each morning from the hen house. There was a problem though. The meanest old rooster guarded that area of the farm and he ruled the roost. He was big - a seemingly larger-than-life rooster, with huge spurs. He would always flog Mamaw, and anyone for that matter that tried to come anywhere near what he had deemed to be his domain. One morning Mamaw was completely fed up with that old rooster attacking her. She picked up a piece of wood from the woodpile and knocked that rooster senseless as it flew towards her. After a few aerobatic flips in the air, he landed lifeless on the ground. Mamaw was horrified as she thought she had killed the family rooster. In those days roosters were not easy to come by and they needed that rooster to ensure they continued hatching new chickens on the farm. She kept it silent and told no one what she had done. Later, that very same day, Mamaw saw the rooster wobbling around the yard like a drunkard. That rooster never again bothered my Mamaw, not once. Seems like a funny story I know, but there is a lesson to be taken here. Most of my Mamaw's life has been spent feeling like that lifeless rooster - like life knocked her senseless and kept her staggering around, not sure of what hit her. When we become courageous and recognize our truest value and identity in Christ, we become the one who knocks the enemy senseless, like my Mamaw knocked that rooster that day. If God be for us – who dare stand against us? God will always triumph over Satan. God will always rule the roost. We must dare to take a stand against the roosters of this world, however! It starts with us. We can be the brave ones, the daring ones, the courageous ones.

I love to make special cakes and treats. I love the freedom to design whimsical creations and love seeing the smiles on the recipient's faces. I love being a part of their special moments in this way. I was recently asked to help cater a baby shower being given for a sweet momma by another organization within our community. This single momma was 33 weeks pregnant with twins. She did not have many resources or life-giving connections. She had seen the flyer for this organization and decided to give it a try. She told us at the baby shower, *"I was not looking for a free baby shower. That is nice, but what I was looking for was a connection and someone to come alongside me and be here with me through this."* That statement ripped a hole right into my very core. She could not have said it any more beautifully or perfectly. This is the cry of our hearts. This is the cry of our Heavenly Father's heart as well. It is our core design. We were created to need others. This is the Father's heart, and why Satan works overtime to pull the plug on the power source. Sadly, this is true in many of our churches as well. The pews (or chairs nowadays) are filled with those who affirm and declare the lie to themselves daily. They are either too busy, too self-absorbed, or too closed off because of past hurts to open themselves up to living in the context of community with others. It is too risky and makes them far too vulnerable. It is not comfortable, but can I share a secret with you? Sometimes, being in community is hard. It is challenging. Perhaps it is supposed to be hard so it sharpens us. It is easy to stay disconnected. The hard work is found in connecting. But like so many other things in life, the best and most wonderful things are often the hardest to obtain.

Let me challenge you today. Get connected. Stay connected. I found 2022 to be one of the most challenging years of our lives personally, yet it also became one of the most refreshing and fulfilling years of our lives. Seems like an oxymoron and complete contradiction I know. It is true though. Tom had one of his toes amputated after a two-year battle of trying to save it, my Dad passed away, Tom's grandpa passed away, and my Aunt passed away. We have entered a new season of challenging health concerns with our parents, dealing with loving adult kiddos through their choices and decisions, as well as dealing with the impact of grief in our new normal after my Dad's home-going. Five years ago, we would have turned to alcohol to numb the pain. Five years ago, we would have shut one another out and nursed our own pain. We now do life with an incredible group of friends we call family. They are life-giving and stand with us. When our vision has been jaded by the pain and exhaustion of life, they are there to hold our hands up and restore clear sight. If Tom and I had not found the power of connectivity and a praying community, we would have been six-feet under today. Satan seeks to isolate us. If he can get us alone on his playing field, make no mistake that his sole purpose will be to take us out. Lack of connection would have cost us everything. It would have cost us our lives, our children, our grandchildren, our community, the impact this ministry has made on thousands of kiddos to date, our families, and our purpose and legacy. It would have cost us our family lineage and mostly, it would have cost us eternity with God. That is a steep price to pay for fear and lack of connectivity. God longs for us to be aligned in purpose, to know truth, and to give of ourselves to others – even when it requires us to give more than we would rather give – or more than we are comfortable giving. It is not about my comfort but His purpose. Connectivity begins with surrender and being willing to live vulnerably with others.

We are better together.
We are stronger together.
We can do this, together.

CHAPTER 15
THE ME THAT NO ONE SEES
So, God – Please Help Me See What You See

In December of 2021, my husband and I took a dream trip to some of the theme parks in Orlando, Florida. He had surprised me with this incredible trip at Christmas. Because I had never been to these theme parks it would be another check off my bucket list and memories made for a lifetime. The past year had been a long and hard year for us *(as many of you can relate)*, eclipsed by the lingering impact and variants of the epidemic, persisting health hurdles with Tom, busyness of crazy schedules, demands of life, and the health concerns of our aging parents. We were unquestionably and even visibly exhausted to those who loved us because of all the stressors we were experiencing. Our chronically busy schedules had revealed our physical, mental, and emotional drain. Despite our efforts to gain more sleep, we could not seem to continue persevering through the season we found ourselves in. We woke up each morning seemingly more tired than the night before when we went to sleep. We slowly became more and more wearied; exhausted to the point we were considering major lifestyle changes that would include walking away from a lot of the work we were doing in the community – our calling for the season of life we were in. This is what the lack of rest will do. Lack of true rest will veil truth with confusion and shroud hearts from hope. Lack of truly resting in God's unforced rhythms to rejuvenate our souls and hearts was robbing Tom and me of joy and purpose. We were struggling to find the balance with everything and everyone demanding a piece of us. Experiencing the very kind of fatigue that more sleep simply could not fix, our mental workstations and emotional processors were jaded, fed-up, and downright worn out. God began to gently whisper a sweet reminder to our spirits - sleep and true rest are not the same thing. Sometimes in our forgetfulness we lump the two together into one category. The commandment to honor the sabbath is for our benefit, not God's. Tom and I needed to slip away with God and each other to turn off the fight or flight mechanism that was screaming – RUN! ESCAPE! I was convinced that living off-grid and adapting a much slower-pace of living was the answer. Choosing to listen to God and actively engage in a time of disconnect from the stressors of our persistently overwhelming life enabled us to reset and refocus.

In each park we rented a scooter for my husband due to the osteomyelitis and tendon issues in his feet. Additionally, we had been approved for a medical pass to aid in our park experience due to both of these medical issues, and because he had a picc line as well. Having the scooter was a blessing that allowed my husband to be in the parks all day. Without his "Batmobile," as we called it, he would not have been able to create this wonderful experience for me. Even in his exhaustion and pain, he was still seeking to serve me. I love his servant heart and I am forever grateful for the time we had together and the memories we made during this trip.

We found out quickly that we might as well have been wearing an invisible cloak, much like the Scimitar's cloaking device over Tatooine engaged by Darth Maul. Our expectations were met in a head-on stealth collision of near cataclysmic proportions on multiple occasions. Sometimes it was as if we were completely invisible, not even there. People walked over us, in front of us, literally pushed us out of the way with their hands, and flat out refused to allow us to pass. There were multiple occasions Tom nearly ran completely over people with his "Batmobile." Our "turning of the other cheek" was on its last legs quite a few times. At one point a park employee, God bless him, saw what was occurring and stepped in front of us to create a path, forced to yell to make his presence known. While at times it was provoking and infuriating, it was also an impressive opportunity to hold tightly to any patience and dignity we had within us. There were many occasions for us to rise higher and remember who we were representing.

I have often felt like this throughout my life. Invisible. Alone. Unseen. Unheard. Disposable and pushed out of the way; screaming to make my presence known - mostly ineffective however. Not deemed worthy enough for others to allow me my rightfully earned position in line, but rather shoved out of the way. Inevitably this led to extreme insecurity and inferiority complexes that would rear their ugly little heads throughout my life. Seeds of anger were deposited deep within me every time I was dismissed or shoved to the side, fortifying the belief I was not good enough, never would be, and might as well shut up and sit down. Every time I felt invalidated, the enemy of my soul would whisper that I had to keep working to prove myself a worthy human and to be accepted by others.

The heart of my Father is an active heart. It does not simply extend Christianese gestures and vocabularies, sending them hurling at me in a grand attempt to impress and wow. His actions speak as loud as His words. He couples His words of truth with actions of love. God moves towards me. He runs towards me when He sees me reaching for Him. He is an engaging Father. He longs to hold me, to carry me, and to bear the weight my human shoulders were never designed to bear. He loves me right where I am. He always sees me. He SEES me in the best times and in the worst times, and He still chooses me every single time. He saw me in my frail humanity when life was literally running over me in a stampede. He saw me – the me the world ignored, the me the world denied, and the me the world shoved to the side. He saw the me that I have abused and neglected. He saw the marred me, scarred and emotionally disfigured because of my own choices and the impact of blunt-force traumas caused by others.

God saw the me that had been dazed by the bureaucracy of an uncaring, relentless, self-absorbed cultural experience. He saw the me sitting on my couch crying in the middle of the night, in complete despair, because my son was once again in a psychiatric hospital. He saw the me drowning my sorrows in a half-gallon of ice cream because I could not seem to process the roller coaster of emotions I was feeling over the turmoil with my son's actions; one moment angry, the next moment completely broken from top to bottom, from tip to toe. He saw the me utterly numbed over the complete destruction of my home in one of my son's violent rages; the me sitting on the steps of my apartment building, all alone with no one. He saw me as I sat in disbelief as what seemed like hundreds of people hung out windows and over balconies as law enforcement and first-responders tried to get into the apartment where my son had barricaded himself. He sat there with me as no one offered a shoulder to lean against. He saw the me who slept with a dead bolt lock on the bedroom door in fear of my own son. He saw the me that was pinned to a wall and dehumanized by my son. He saw the me unable to sleep because I was afraid at any moment, in the middle of the night, the repo-ninjas were going to show up and take off with my vehicle. He saw the me that had been abandoned by friends because they could no longer handle the drama in my life. He saw the me that looked to fill the hole in my heart and numb the pain with everything from food, to addictions, to relationships, to excessive shopping, to thrill seeking. He saw the lonely me – the destitute, depleted, and drained me that simply wanted to go to sleep and not ever wake up again. He saw the me that desperately wanted to be loved and to love, and would have done absolutely anything to receive that love. He saw the me that tried to be the best mom she could, yet seemed to fail anew each and every day, never reaching the unattainable bar. AND - it all broke His heart. His heart broke with mine.

The heart of my Father, as Lisa Harper describes in her Devotional Book, *LIFE – An Obsessively Grateful, Undone by Jesus, Genuinely Happy, And Not Faking It Through the Hard Stuff Kind of 100-Day Devotional*, is *"moved by the wounds of humanity."* My appearance does not scare God. My condition does not scare God. My oozing injuries do not send Him running like a silly school girl who just saw a spider or snake on the playground. My scars are not a turnoff to Him. Lisa Harper goes on to express, *"Our ache accelerates His compassion. He intentionally reaches out to restore us when we find ourselves filthy and ashamed before Him."* How beautiful is this! This thought. Think about for a minute. Can't you just see it? When I am swallowed up in my aches, in my discouragement, in depression, in desperation, in the fear of the unknown – that accelerates God's warmth and love, His tenderness and reach, His care and concern, His benevolence and consideration towards me. He accelerates – increasing in His amount of extent. My condition does not turn Him away. Contrary to my understanding, He rushes towards me when I fix my eyes on Him. In another words, HE becomes greater than everything else that is attempting to take me down and out. He increases and all the other junk decreases because I am His child and I have cried out to Him. Can you see it now? His warmth and love swallow up pain and discouragement. His tender reach holds me close and cradles me like a mom with her newborn infant. His gentleness pours into my wounds as a salve and begins to bring healing. He fills my lungs with new breath when I have been knocked breathless. Just like that park employee who put himself into our situation, stepping into our reality, and making his authority trump everything else – this is a picture-perfect description of the love of God stepping into the middle of our brokenness.

Our Bible is a living, breathing revelation of the undeniable fact that our God is LOVE. Everything is tempered with and by this immense great LOVE. Everything has a foundation in this unfailing LOVE. Everything known and unknown in the natural and spiritual is rooted in, founded in, provided by, and finished by His great, unconditional, overwhelming, without flaw, incredible, reliable, and infatuating LOVE. His amazing LOVE is exhaustive, thorough, comprehensive, and complete. This was displayed so beautifully and illustrated so excellently as God our Father sent His one and only Son to earth. This is beautifully illustrated where in His becoming part of humanity and living as a man, Jesus Christ sacrificed Himself in a cruel, underserved, and harrowing manner. He then rose again – demonstrating this immeasurable act of His GREAT LOVE for us! AND, when He comes again – and He will come again - that will be the final fulfillment of His GREAT LOVE for us. I have not always thought of myself as one deserving of love like this, but John 3:16-18 tells both you and me otherwise. I love The Message Translation (MSG) of this passage of scriptures:

"This is how much God loved the world: He gave his Son, his one and only Son. And this is why: so that no one need be destroyed; by believing in him, anyone can have a whole and lasting life. God didn't go to all the trouble of sending his Son merely to point an accusing finger, telling the world how bad it was. He came to help, to put

the world right again. Anyone who trusts in him is acquitted; anyone who refuses to trust him has long since been under the death sentence without knowing it. And why? Because of that person's failure to believe in the one-of-a-kind Son of God when introduced to him."

In late 2018, the crumbled ruins of what was left of my life were presented in an act of complete surrender and submission before God, and ultimately laid at the foot of the Cross. Jesus cleared the rubble and brought beauty from the ashes. He demolished the old structures I had erected and built a new infrastructure on a steady and firm foundation. This is how much God loves me. This is how much God loves you. Anyone can have this promise. This truth. This life principle. We need only trust and surrender; a daily choice to choose surrender over resistance. God longs to be the cloud that covers us by day, the fire that leads us and warms us in the night, the rear-guard that protects us, the foundation and cornerstone that supports us, and the manna that sustains us. Will we allow Him to be?

My life is dotted with moments when I would provisionally surrender my all on the altar of defeat. I would declare my total bankrupt status and complete dependency upon God. Then, being the great re-possessor I am, I would repeatedly take back the sacrifices I had made - although not always consciously or deliberately. The back-and-forth yo-yo of my life, in every season and every area can be clearly documented. You know what else is visible though? The moment I began to clearly understand. The moment I fully and whole-heartedly embraced the beauty and essence of an absolute and unreserved daily surrender. This seismic faith recognized its 100% dependency upon God and surrendered self-reliance. Life on my terms was unequivocally exasperating and exhausting. I will forever be grateful for a Father who sees me, for a Father who knows me, and for a Father who still chooses me every single moment of every single day despite the ups and downs. I was a very broken daughter of a King who did not know her own worth. I needed a realignment. I needed the spiritual blinders removed. There's a story I love tucked away in 2nd Kings 6. I find myself captivated when I imagine this in my mind's eye.

Early in the morning a servant of the Holy Man got up and went out. Surprise! Horses and chariots surrounding the city! The young man exclaimed, "Oh, master! What shall we do? He said, "Don't worry about it—there are more on our side than on their side." Then Elisha prayed, "O God, open his eyes and let him see." The eyes of the young man were opened and he saw. A wonder! The whole mountainside full of horses and chariots of fire surrounding Elisha! When the Arameans

attacked, Elisha prayed to God, "Strike these people blind!" And God struck them blind, just as Elisha said.
2 Kings 6: 15-18 The Message Translation (MSG)

How I see my situation, my circumstances, and others will determine the trajectory of my life. When I only see what I can see in the natural I will often misinterpret the reality of what the truth is. This will lead me down a path of deception. It is only when I allow God to open my eyes and remove the blinders that I can see what God sees. In our text we see that the enemy had surrounded Elisha. All his servant could see was defeat. He could not see a way out. Elisha saw the situation differently though. Elisha filtered his view through a different lens. He had already pre-determined that fear had no place in his life, and therefore he would not be ruled and governed by fear. Elisha prayed and asked God to open the eyes of his servant so he too could see that the enemy was outnumbered by a long shot.

I did not like what I saw when I looked at my life. I remember crying out to God one evening and asking Him, *"If this must be my life, if I must travel this path, can you please just make it as easy as possible. I am so tired."* In 2018, I hated my life. I told God I hated my life. I made sure God knew how I felt. I held nothing back from Him. The truth is, I may not like what I see, but that does not mean that I must accept what I see. I can stand on the authority of Jesus

Christ and I can reject what I see in the natural with my human eyes. I can ask God to open the eyes of my understanding to see His bigger God picture. When I process life through the lens of Jesus, it becomes easy to see that the enemy of our souls is far outnumbered.

I am married today to a wonderful man who makes my heart smile bigger than a sugar junkie standing in front of a donut display at Krispy Kreme. God has given me more than I deserve. He radically changed Tommy and me through the gift of complete surrender. The ability to choose surrender is the greatest gift. The ability to see through the lens of Christ is like the lyrics of an old hymn, *"Thank You Lord for Your Blessings on Me"* by the Easter Brothers:

> **There's a roof up above me**
> **I've a good place to sleep**
> **There's food on my table**
> **And shoes on my feet**
> **You gave me your love Lord**
> **And a fine family**
> **Thank you Lord**
> **For your blessings on me**

Every day we have been given a gift. We have the opportunity to ask God to open our eyes, to help us to see what He sees, and to blind the eyes of our enemies. Every day we can choose to look through God's lens and view life through His eyes. It is our choice. We get to choose. Opportunity is given, so why not take it?

CHAPTER 16
IMPRINTING
God's Trademark and Signature Stamp

The process of imprinting is rather unique. It requires the softer substance conform to the formation of the harder substance being pressed into it. Over the past several years my life has been a mirrored image of a story found tucked away in the book of Exodus. Without a doubt I know that God is a very visible banner over my life today. In my imperfection, in my failure, and in my exhaustion, I began to desire to reflect the image of my creator. There in those moments I began to see His banner flying over my life in ways that were undeniably God. Just like the day that the Israelites prevailed in victory over the Amalekites, so it is with my life. My life commemorated and remembered as one marked by the trademark of God – A life that is clearly visible by the banner flying overhead as a symbol that God is with me.

We are made in the image of the Great I AM. Because of this we are of immense value and worth to Him. God's fingerprints are upon every fiber of our being; His likeness stamped upon our hearts for all eternity. The fabrics and tapestries of our very lives are embossed with His creativity and beautiful inspiration of hope and love. He has literally inscribed Himself upon us. He is for us! What an encouraging revelation! We must find the courage within to believe this truth.

If you take a ball of playdough and press a coin into it, the image of that coin will be replicated in the playdough. This process of an outline of the harder subject being reproduced in the surface of the softer substance is what we know as imprinting. This same process can be seen in the animal kingdom when a young animal comes to recognize another animal or person as their parent or an object of considerable and significant trust. We could also say that imprinting is like a signature, a banner, a design, an indentation, a stamp, or a trademark. This is where I want to settle in – I love this story and all that it represents.

And Moses built an altar and called the name of it – The Lord Is my Banner! Exodus 17:15 ESV

When the children of Israel faced the Amalekites, it did not take much to see they were ill-equipped by natural human calculations. They were not fierce warriors decked out in state-of-the-art armor and weaponry. The children of Israel were a simple people, ordinary by human account – everyday men, women, and children with herds of animals and all their possessions in tow – delivered from slavery with an expectation of a promised land of hope. Yet, they found themselves faced with a fierce enemy in a battle for their very existence; a battle for their survival. Does this sound familiar? Does this sound like your life? Well, by this point you undoubtably know it definitely sounds like my life! The children of Israel possessed something their adversaries did not however. A treasure their enemy did not have access to, and something the enemy was not counting on - they had God's presence with them. His likeness was imprinted on them and, therefore, they were not alone. They were anything but ordinary – and my friends, we are anything but ordinary. How can we be ordinary when our Father is extraordinary?

We are children of the One True GOD! That makes us a majority. If God be for us, then who dare have the audacity to attempt standing against us? If they succeed in forming weapons, their weapons will never prevail against the Lord of the Angel Armies. When it looks like we are surrounded, we simply take inventory of what we know to be truth. God is with us! We take our battle position of prayer, worship, and obedience. The children of Israel would not fight their enemy – the enemy of God – alone. This battle was not about their abilities or their qualifications, although I am certain at times, they were asking God, *"HEY GOD – ARE YOU SURE? HEY GOD – GOD – WHOO – HOOO - DO YOU SEE WHAT'S GOING ON DOWN HERE?"* I am certain at some point they felt this promised land of hope was a long shot and they had little chance of winning. I'm sure they felt unprepared, insufficient, and lacking in skill-sets for the enormous adversary that lay in front of them. I can only but imagine how they must have felt, taking a stand on the outside while feeling exhausted and discouraged on the inside – the underdogs who were no match for the mighty warriors before them – warriors that stood between them and hope and promise. Have you ever felt like this? Have you ever felt that despite your best efforts, nothing was ever going to be enough?

I can recall standing in my living room one day nearly ten years ago now - distraught and unable to calm my raging emotions. I screamed at the ceiling that represented everything that was separating me from peace, *"When is enough going to be enough God? Take one of us out of our misery, please. Why can't this be easier?"* I heard God clearly respond that day, *"Easier for who? Easier for you? Or, what is best for your son? Will you trust me?"* Those days were not easy. They were some of the hardest days I have ever known. I didn't want to walk the path I found myself on. I felt like the underdog. I felt weak. I felt ill-equipped and overwhelmingly exhausted. I was angry that life had to be this hard. I was jealous of the relationships I saw other parents enjoy with their children. Their lives didn't seem to be as hard as mine. As much as I have openly shared, there are some moments I have yet to find words to describe. I was experiencing a level of exhaustion that sleep could not fix, a level of fatigue I wasn't certain I'd ever come out of. My son's mental illness, coupled with his manipulative tendencies and violent nature, left little to be desired in life. Friends and family had distanced themselves. Every day was spent in survival mode. Every day was spent trying to keep the scales balanced. God wanted me to trust Him in the midst of the chaos. God wanted me to see what He saw, not what my circumstances dictated and were showing me. I found myself screaming the same thing, *"HEY GOD – ARE YOU SURE? HEY GOD – GOD – WHOO – HOOO - DO YOU SEE WHAT'S GOING ON DOWN HERE?"*

The children of Israel saw God as someone in whom they could place great trust. When you have God's presence with you, you are never alone – you are never the underdog, even though in the natural you may feel like it. You are never at a loss when God is with you. To place your trust in God does not mean you are never "fearful." It is not about our ability to stand fearless, or about our capacity and propensity to be anything, for that matter. It is not by our power or strength, but His power that gives us courage and boldness to go forth with the marching orders He gives us – despite our human shortcomings and imperfections. It is only through Him that we can do or be anything. It is only through Him we are able to stand bold and valiant through perfect love. The name used in Scripture to describe our God in moments like these is Jehovah-Nissi – THE LORD IS MY BANNER. His love over me, His strength over me, His peace over me, His provision over me, His protection over me – His presence over me is a Banner! A victory banner! This is what Moses was declaring! This is the journey God was taking me on. He was imprinting Himself upon my heart.

He is the God of the Angel Armies. He is our shield and mighty fortress. I think we sometimes struggle with picturing this battle stance in today's society because we aren't physically lined up on a battle field with a sword and shield in hand. God is the ruling general of the massive heavenly squadron sent to annihilate our foes. It may look like we are surrounded by darkness, but with God (the light) there can be no complete darkness. Sometimes the battles we face in life seem to rage on forever. They are layer upon layer upon layer, stacked into miles-high cumulative piles that have become overwhelming and inconceivable. We see no end in sight. We grow weary, feeling drained and sapped, we start sagging and lagging – mentally fatigued with a weight too heavy for us to carry alone. This is where I found myself nearly ten years ago, and it would take a journey of another six years for me to finally grasp what God so desperately wanted me to understand. Sometimes God will affront our minds to arrest our hearts. He cares far more about the condition and position of our hearts that anything we think we know to be truth about our situations.

This is exactly what God did to me. He interrupted my observances and cognizance to show me a truth I never knew I needed.

This story in Exodus is a vision of redemption and salvation; of hope and promise – a story of God's faithfulness to always be with us and fight on our behalf when we stay the course. We must keep our eyes on Him, even when we do not understand and we cannot clearly see. When we cannot see Him working, we must choose to trust His nature. He is the author and finisher of our faith. That sounds so cliché – and if you have grown up in church, then you have heard that phrase a million-plus times. BUT – as cliché as we may think it sounds – it is Scripture and it is TRUTH! It is an absolute truth! It is a truth we should embrace and become intimate with. This is the truth that will set us free once we KNOW it – once we apply it. This story in Exodus paints a picture of wisdom, as we begin to see that strength is found together within the concept of connectivity and community. We were never meant to do life alone as we have already discussed. God designed life to be done in the context of relationships. As Aaron and Hur realized what was taking place, they stepped in with support to uphold Moses when he was growing tired and weak – in the moment he found himself battle weary and worn. This was a battle that seemed to have no end as it went on...and on...and on, like a very bad audition for American Idol or The Voice.

My husband and I found ourselves in this very same type of battle with his health. This battle would ultimately lead to a toe amputation after a two-year painful fight. I am certain our stance would be vastly different without the community of friends and family who have surrounded us over the past five years. I was also in this same type of battle with my son. Aaron and Hur recognized the need and without being asked they moved a boulder for Moses to sit upon. Then they each took one of his arms and held it up. It was TOGETHER that they became mighty again. Victorious! The Israelite fighters rallied around Joshua in their renewed strength provoking fear upon their enemy. It was TOGETHER they reminded one another that God was the trademark of their lives and success. TOGETHER my husband and I will face any battles before us knowing that God is within us and we are surrounded by a community to help us. We are stronger TOGETHER.

In our story in Exodus, we find the battle continued to rage throughout the day and into the night. Have you ever felt like this? Have you ever felt so battle-weary that you could not take another step forward – so tired you stopped caring about any and everything? I have! I know this place. Perhaps, like Joshua, you have felt overwhelmed at the immense pressure of everyone looking to you for orders and direction. You feel you cannot measure up to their expectations, or perhaps even that you have nothing left to give to anyone. You are empty. Perhaps you have felt like Moses – that you need to remain strong for everyone looking to you for answers – your family, your spouse, your co-workers, your community, your employees, your children, or your students. Perhaps you have grown weary from standing in the gap for others. You have begun to lose sight of victory from sheer exhaustion. You feel the pressure that if you fail, all those looking to you will fail also. You are carrying the weight of the world upon your shoulders, and the rise or fall of success is dependent upon your ability and capacity to remain untouched by the war that is raging. This is why it is critically important to prioritize doing this thing we call "life" together with like-minded people. Surrounding ourselves with those who are on the same path as we are strengthens our resolve and equips us to withstand during hardships. Surrounding ourselves with like-minded people who are observant and watching out for anything seeking to cause defeat is part of a strategic life plan. Living within this context gives us the mental, physical, and emotional bandwidth needed to keep up the good fight when the harsh realities of living are thrown at us.

Although life is a beautiful gift, life is also unsympathetic to our plights. At times life seems hell-bent on breaking us, and like the Amalekite army, set on completely taking us out. If Satan can isolate us, then he has us on his playing field. Do not be deceived and make no mistake, he will take you out. Do not allow yourself to walk through life alone. Scripture tells us this battle, this day, was a day to be remembered. It became part of their legacy and lineage. It was a day that left a mark, an impression upon the hearts and minds of all who were there; of those who even heard about it. I want my life to be a life that is remembered and makes a mark, an impact on all that come after me. What is your game-changing strategy? Walking with God in the protective layer of community that He designed is a game-changer! The people prevailed against their enemy because God was with them and they stood TOGETHER. God was imprinted on their hearts and lives – and that image was visible to all who saw it – and they were committed to God and to each other. It was clear. It was a proclamation of God's faithfulness and goodness. Moses kept his focus fixed on God because he knew God was their source of success, hope, and promise. It was not easy by any stretch of the imagination. What's best in life is not always what is easiest in life.

So, what did Moses actually mean when he said *"The Lord is my Banner!"*?

My children and I used to love watching the Macy's Thanksgiving Day Parade every year. The grand magnitude of extravagance on full display was mesmerizing and exciting. I loved the bands the most. Out in front of each band would be a banner that identified where they were from. These banners were clearly distinctive as a representation. Banners are used to identify, to honor, to celebrate, and to pay tribute to those who are deserving. Banners are used to promote and are highly recognizable – visible. Banners are used as proclamations and notifications. We hang them from rafters, between trees, attach them to buildings and billboards, or fly them from flag poles. Banners are unmistakably noticeable and their sole intent is to be seen by as many people as possible, from as far away as possible. Can you see it now? Can you see why Moses called God a Banner over him? Can you see God as a Banner over your life? Is God's trademark and signature stamp upon your life visible to all who encounter you?

As spiritual revelations begin to deposit the truth of God into our hearts about our core identity, and as we begin to fully understand our immense value and worth as a child of God, then we begin to understand that God never intended for us to fight these battles and enemies of life on our own. He has provided everything we will ever need through our relationships with others and through our proximity to Him. God does not just give us strength. God does not just give us peace. God does not just give us hope. God is the very essence of these things. And this my friend – this reality is the game-changer.

He is STRENGTH!
He is PEACE!
He is HOPE!

The weapons of our warfare are not carnal. They are made of something not of this world. They are mighty for the pulling down of strongholds and enemies set on completely taking us out in life. There is a very real enemy of our souls. But there is one greater than our adversary.

You are of God, little children, and have overcome them, because He who is in you is greater than he who is in the world. 1 John 4:4 MEV

I stand in awe of how God has imprinted Himself upon my life through the access I gave to Him; how Heaven has literally kissed my existence. It is nothing short of a miracle that I am here on this early Sunday morning able to type out these words. I have not always carried the signature of God upon my life, even though I grew up in church. Because of the condition of my calloused heart, His indention was not always evident to those I encountered. Through deep heartache, pain, hurt, and regret I have learned to fix my focus on the very one who has always been the source of my strength, hope, and peace. I have learned to surround myself with those in life who will lift me up in times when I am weak and weary. I have learned to allow God to soften my callouses and gently massage my broken heart back to life. By natural design I am an introvert – a trait only my closest of friends and family know about me. I feel completely at ease with doing life alone – but that is a playground for the enemy and certainly not the way God designed life to be lived. I often require times of withdrawal to recharge my drained batteries. I enjoy these times of retreat and aloneness, but constantly am guarded to keep it within balance. We are stronger together.

If all of us are honest, life is just messy and downright ugly sometimes. It can suck the breath right out of us. We must lay aside our pride however and get real, guys. Like many of you, I have felt the weight and overwhelming pressures and stressors of life. I know what it is like to have the piercing judgment of the world reigning down on me. I know what it feels like to be so ashamed and embarrassed, so hurt and distraught, that you want to go to bed and never get up. I also know what it is like to find God pressing into me, making His indention into my heart and soul – and in that moment I had a choice – a choice to allow it or to pull away. A choice to remain soft and pliable, or to become hard and rigid. There is immense beauty that words cannot describe found in a life trademarked by His remarkable presence. As I reached, He reached. As I established myself in His ways, He established Himself in me. As I took baby steps towards Him, He was there as a loving Father cheering me on and reaching out to me, as if I were a wobbly toddler learning to walk. In my imperfection I began to desire to reflect the image of my Creator. There in those moments I began to see His banner flying over my life in ways that were undeniably God. Just like the day that the Israelites prevailed in victory over the Amalekites, so it is with my life – My life to be remembered as one marked by the trademark of God – A life that is clearly visible by the banner flying overhead as a symbol that God is with me. God is literally blotting out the enemies of my life from under heaven – from existence. If God be for me – Who dare stand against me?! Is this your trademark? Is God's love and faithfulness a banner over your life?

CHAPTER 17
MY STORY, HIS STORY

The Merriam-Webster online dictionary defines the word "fake" as something that is not true, real, or genuine. My husband and I often go on antiquing road trips. We love it. My husband is an avid collector of Westmoreland Glass and has been for years. Collecting this glassware is a hobby he has shared with his eldest son since he was a teenager, and to this day they love the adrenaline rush of the search and find. Their relationship has been enriched greatly through their shared interest of collecting Westmoreland treasures, which is highly sought after by many collectors as it is no longer in production.

Our home is filled many treasures Tommy has found over the years, as well as some we have found together. My favorites, hands down, must be the Westmoreland pure white milk glass and the frosted strawberry collection. They are a perfect companion to my modern farmhouse meets vintage farmhouse kitchen and house décor. When I first started learning about Westmoreland, I found it hard to identify the imposters from the authentic pieces. Tommy seemed to be able to spot a fake from a mile away. However, as I have gained a deeper knowledge of Westmoreland's rich history and incredible artistry displayed in all of their works, I am far less likely to be tripped up by counterfeits nowadays.

Raising my son was not a task for the weak at heart. Loving Eli was not for the gentle and easily imposed upon spirit. I now intentionally give thanks to God for entrusting me with the privilege of loving Eli. It was not always easy however. I discovered I would be required to discover the balance of loving Eli with an open heart, open arms, and open hands in ways I never knew existed. I had to take everything I thought I knew about love and toss it out the window, allowing God to reformat my mind. I had to check my understanding at the door and seek to absorb a greater awareness of the truest meaning of God's love.

I learned I would need to love Eli from a distance while I allowed and trusted God to hold him. I learned what it meant to love him even in the moments I could not stand being around him; when I did not understand or agree with his choices and preferences. That is a tough statement to process. It is a difficult position for any parent to be in. No parent likes to admit they do not like their child. It has often felt like a spiritual battle raging whenever I would be in my son's presence; the spirit within me at odds with the spirit inside of him. At times I have felt like the worst parent in the world – after all, what kind of parent does not accept their own child. Satan used this lie to immobilize me many times until I finally understood that my not accepting and agreeing with my son's actions and choices did not mean I did not love him. True love is not declared through an absolute compliance with the poor choices of others. That is not true love at all, but rather enabling. My choosing to not allow nor tolerate Eli's miscalculations, vicious displays of anger, and improper choices had absolutely nothing to do with my love for him, and certainly did not mean I wasn't choosing him. Choosing to draw healthy boundary lines does not mean we are not available to our son and present in his life – helping when appropriate, encouraging when needed, guiding as allowed, and offering wisdom when sought.

I learned the moments Eli fell the hardest were the moments he would need me the most. In these moments when everyone else in life abandoned him, I was reminded of what it is like to be held by our Heavenly Father when we have crashed and burned ourselves. I learned how to love Eli through my pain, as my heart was shattering into a million tiny pieces and spreading across the landscape of this thing called life. I learned that I would need to simply love him without being able to manipulate and control the outcome to turn in the direction I desired. I learned I would have to trust through the blind spots; learning to love Eli even when I could not see him, or see how the ash pile could ever be redeemed. That would be mandatory for beauty to rise from the ashes. I learned keeping my eyes focused on where I wanted to go instead of the hurdle in front of me would be paramount to survival and overcoming.

Loving Eli would require that I become an expert in being assertive in my love. It would require I not allow myself to become easily manipulated and as a result become his puppet. I had to learn how to love with parameters and healthy boundaries in place. Most therapists agree that these are good mechanisms for coping and healthy strategies for successful living. In many cases – they are! When you are raising a mentally ill and often violent child on your own however, the status-quo, cookie-cutter, broiler plate pieces of advice do not always work. In fact, they often do not work. They are not one-size fits all.

Eli was never what I defined as a neuro-typical child. He never "played by the rules" or fit into societal pre-made molds of acceptance. Loving and raising Eli would require many sacrifices time and time again; sacrifices that only a parent would selflessly offer over and over. It would mandate the development of personal and spiritual resiliency that would act as a reinforcement to the flexibility I needed. The ability to remain unwavering in the face of a proposed hopelessness and helplessness, and becoming elastic and pliable in my ability to respond to the daily roadblocks, would be crucial to maintaining my own mental and physical health. I gave my all and at times it never seemed to be enough. It has only been in the past three to four years that I have grown to understand that I did not fail as a parent and I did not fail my child. Some of life's hardest realities have no words to be found in which understanding can be given. I have learned that sometimes things just are. I cannot control and manipulate the outcomes because I cannot control and manipulate others. Learning to ride the waves without drowning in the power of those waves is a journey many do not survive. The story of my son Eli is one such story.

When you become efficient in bending with whichever way the wind may be blowing each day, living an authentic life becomes more and more unrecognizable. I began to always anticipate the next violent outburst, always looking over my shoulder, and always wondering when the hammer would fall again. I would try to believe the best. I would try to only think good, positive, life-giving thoughts. I would try so very hard to believe the next time it would be different, yet it never was. I found myself growing angry over the amount of energy exhausted on trying to survive, energy that took away from my relationship with my daughter, robbed me of family, and stole friendships.

The resourcefulness that becomes a person's survival guide in situations like this serves a dual purpose to also disable and disarm them from living a life of authenticity. This was my story. My own resourcefulness taught me not to let my guard down or be vulnerable, because letting my guard down could end disastrously as it had many times before. Letting my guard down meant I could end up injured, or worse. There were two occasions when my son tried to wreck the car while I was driving it, attacking me like a wild animal. My resourcefulness taught me to put on a smile, wear the mask, pretend I was okay when truthfully, I was dying inside. Many people in our lives walked away, and many more would if they knew the reality of what I was walking through with Eli at the time. It was difficult for my own family to handle the veracity of life with Eli and therefore I never had much respite. Often, I felt invisible and abandoned. I went years where the only breathers I would receive would be when he was in an inpatient psychiatric ward, or being held in juvenile detention for domestic violence against me and violating the terms of his parole.

The list of labels and diagnoses were not near as long as the cocktails of medications we would try. The Merriam-Webster online dictionary describes "resilience" as the ability of an elastic material (such as rubber) to absorb energy (such as from a blow) and release that energy as it springs back to its original shape. Over the years I began absorbing the shock waves my son sent out, but somewhere along the way I lost the ability to release it and spring back into shape. I became tired. I became weak. I became weary. I started to lose the gentle spirit that I was once known by. I became harsh. I became cynical. I became critical. I became easily overwhelmed and incapable of handling stressors of any sorts. This is what loving my son did to me and I felt ashamed that I was not better and stronger. I felt like a horrible parent – but, this was my definition of love. This is how I defined love and my definition was very flawed. God defines love very differently.

I cannot separate who I am from what I do when everything I do is done as unto the Lord. I cannot compartmentalize my life into categories of deeds, actions, and works in one bucket and faith and beliefs in another. To do so feels fake; unauthentic. To do so feels like I am cheating myself and God. I spent more than half of my life trying to measure up and be good enough, only to be brutally reminded time and time again that I would never be enough or be able to do enough; only to be reminded repeatedly that I'd always fall short of the imaginary line I created marking the spot of "arrival". It is not by works lest man should boast. This is a powerful nugget of truth tucked deep into the Holy Scripture. Works will never lead to my salvation, worth, value, and acceptance, but salvation should lead to works as I reflect the image of my Creator. So often we get sideways in our understanding of this. My identity, worth, and value are not determined by how much

I do, but rather it is based in the undeniable truth of who God says I am through His son Jesus. I do not have to carry the cross of proving myself every single day to earn my position, His attention, or His stamp of approval upon my existence. I had been trying to prove that I was not a failure as a mother - over and over and over - every single minute of every single hour of every single day - and, I failed. I failed over and over and over again because I neglected to remember that none of this was based on my performance and ability. The Cross of Jesus was and is enough.

I have come to believe and understand that I will only ever discover God's will for my life within the explicit context of His will for mankind, eternity, and the earth I call my temporary home. His will is clear, obvious, and unequivocal; indisputably precise in detail. I am made for HIS story; existing to play a role (my story) in the framework of the bigger story (His story) – or else I would not exist at all. I have a purpose and that purpose lies within His purpose. He is course-plotting, navigating me through the storms of life – storms that entered God's perfect design through the evil of sin. We live in a fallen world because of this sin, yet God is everywhere, in every second of every moment, working all things for the good of those who are in relationship with Him. I can guarantee you that life will not happen on my terms. It will not happen on your terms either. I have tried. I have failed miserably. Chances are – you have tried and failed too. The outcomes will not always look the way I would like them to. Yet, there is one thing that is true – this one thing I know. God is for me. God is good. God is good to me. As Chris Tomlin's song beautifully declares – He's a Good, Good Father, That's Who He Is. And I'm Loved by Him, That's Who I am.

We pray for God to break our hearts for what breaks His, yet we've a very vague understanding of what actually breaks His heart. So often I have prayed in ignorance, yet God still loves me and sees my heart's desire. We pray for God to remove our pain and suffering. We pray and pray, and when we feel we have not been heard, we grow angry and distant. We have carefully, and very creatively constructed our God-boxes where we store concepts and ideas of how we perceive God to work, move, and exist among us. I must submit to you the idea that God is very well acquainted with our humanity, seeing as we are created in His image. There is not a single emotion we experience that He cannot understand. He is a veteran of every hurt, pain, disappointment, fear, and suffering we will ever walk through in this life.

God has a will and we simply cannot see the big picture yet of how it all unfolds in an instant. Our job is to live authentically and in obedient surrender, even when we cannot see or understand. Life has taught me that God gives and He takes away. Life is full of joy and wonder, and yet we also experience great pain, disappointment, and suffering. Many moments of my life are dotted with fragments of deep pain and regret that I had rather never happened. It was not my plan. It was not my intention. There were many unmet expectations and unrealized dreams and hopes that never came into fruition the way I saw them playing out in my mind. God's love letters to us reveal part of His glory and plan, but it is possible we may never fully know this side of Heaven how our suffering plays a part in His story; or maybe we will. That is for Him to determine, not us.

Sometimes God may call us to patiently and with perseverance till dirt. That is what raising Eli felt like. I felt like I was constantly tilling the dirt, yet never getting to plant a seed or see a harvest. I have come to a place of resolve where I have decided to simply be "okay" with not knowing until I see God face-to-face; understanding that someday I will have answers to how my story was weaved into His great story – or perhaps someday on the other side of eternity I will not need answers anymore, because I'll all at once understand. There is a thought to ponder on for a while.

And we know [with great confidence] that God [who is deeply concerned about us] causes all things to work together [as a plan] for good for those who love God, to those who are called according to His plan and purpose. Romans 8:28 Amplified (AMP)

Despite the outward circumstances and situations of our lives, we can still serve God and live an authentic and heart-felt life with cheerful anticipation of playing a role in God's bigger story. Confidence brings a level of freedom and happiness that only exist through deep, intimate, and authentic relationship with Christ.

...in every situation [no matter what the circumstances] be thankful and continually give thanks to God; for this is the will of God for you in Christ Jesus. 1 Thessalonians 5:18 Amplified (AMP)

Our pain in life is not joyful in and of itself. We are not instructed to be thankful for all things, rather in all things to extend thankfulness to our Father who is working on our behalf. Everything that happens to a child of God in this life is overruled by God and used by Him for the greater good of ALL– for His story and His purpose and His will – and this is how the will and purpose of our lives is part of His will and purpose for all mankind. Nothing happens to me unless it first passes through the hands of God.

For this reason, I will never waste a hurt again. I will never allow pain and grief to render me inoperative. That does not mean there will not be a temporary paralysis, but what it does mean is that I will not walk through the valley of the shadow of death alone. The very fact there is a shadow points out that light is present. Jesus will be there with me, taking every step with me.

So, here is a thought – **what if my greatest purpose and calling, the greatest gift I could ever give the world and God** (my purpose in life), **what if it was hidden within and tangled up inside my darkest and most painful moments?** What if out of my greatest adversities come my greatest triumphs; the moments I wish had never happened becoming the catapult for purpose and legacy. The moments I wish would disappear becoming a survival guide pointing others to Jesus. The moments I want to run from and hide from becoming light in the dark for someone on the edge barely hanging on. What if your greatest purpose is this too? This is how God weaves our story into His story for all mankind. We need one another. We need connection. We need community. The greatest gift ever given to mankind was amidst great torture and suffering as Jesus willingly died in agony upon the Cross. It was the darkest hour of our history. He prayed if it would be the will of His Father that this purpose of His life be changed and that He would be delivered from this path of suffering and agony. What if our scars in life, the very things that have wounded us to the point of devastation, leaving us beyond recognition at times, what if those things point to the greater story – HIS STORY? What if this is our purpose? To love God. To love others. To serve God. To serve others. To live authentically and out loud before others. For our lives - the good, the bad, and the ugly - to point to the Cross – what if this is our ultimate purpose and destiny?

We can choose to be bitter or better about the circumstances of our lives. We can choose to live joy-filled regardless of outward temporal circumstances – realizing that true joy is not conjured up from an outward positioning, but rather from an inward relationship with Christ. We can choose to allow the unpredictable nature of life to transform us into the image of our Creator, or we can allow it to make us hostile and skeptical towards everything and everyone we encounter. Do we truly believe that our life's story is part of God's greater story for all mankind? There is no middle ground. We either believe God's word is truth and life, or we do not!

If we make God a last resort to the experiences of life, we will never fully understand the context of Romans 8:28. God must be the first response. BUT GOD! Joseph spent 20 years suffering before he would be used as part of God's plan to save his nation. His suffering did not seem fair. It did not seem right. It was dark. It was lonely. He was abandoned. His brothers despised him so much they sold him into slavery and told his father he had been killed. Can you imagine that level of rejection and pain? Everything familiar was stripped from him. Then just when Joseph thought it could not possibly get any worse, it did. Another lie was cast upon him and he was thrown into prison – it was unfair, unjust, and painful – yet Joseph never stopped trusting and honoring God. He continued to be authentic. He never stopped believing despite the hardship. He remained full of integrity even as it seemed he was forgotten and alone. His darkest moments were simply a setup for God's destiny to unfold in his life.

In his suffering, Joseph remained faithful in his beliefs. He remained steadfast in his relationship in the closeness of his proximity with God. Joseph believed that God had a purpose for his suffering, although he could not see the bigger picture of how this suffering played a part in the bigger story of God's will and purpose for mankind. My skin crawls every time I hear someone make the statement – "All we can do is pray now." God was not a last resort for Joseph, where he chose to pray after trying everything else. It was through his physical, mental, and emotional agony that many lives would be saved. When we love GOD FIRST, all things work together – all things are weaved together – all things are connected and operate in unity as one in purpose for the will of the Father. This is the heart of God. God does not simply show up after the fact trying to somehow make sense of the chaos – trying to fit it into His plan and work it out to benefit us. For those who love God, who are in relationship with God, God is there from the beginning. He is there when the suffering occurs to begin with. He is there at every moment of the suffering. None of it takes Him by surprise.

As for you, you meant evil against me, but God meant it for good in order to bring about this present outcome, that many people would be kept alive [as they are this day]. Genesis 50:20 Amplified (AMP)

This calls for a deeper level of understanding of the true meaning of GOD IS IN CONTROL. His ways and thoughts are higher than ours. There are times in life that we are not going to understand what is happening, why it is happening, the purpose of it happening, or even the fairness of what is happening. I examined my own life and the battles we faced with our son. It is heartbreaking. It is not the path we would have chosen. It is not the path we desired. We still do not like it. Yet, in these moments there is peace because we know God is weaving even "this" into the bigger image of HIS story. One day we will see and understand. Before time began, before our son was even a thought in my mind or a seed in my belly, God looked down through all eternity and saw this very moment. If I believe His word in Jeremiah 29:11, then I must believe that God has been there from the beginning, through every moment of our lives, and even right this very moment is standing with us.

For I know the plans and thoughts that I have for you, says the LORD, plans for peace and well-being and not for disaster, to give you a future and a hope. Jeremiah 29:11 Amplified (AMP)

I cannot cherry pick and choose which part of Scripture I will believe and not believe. I cannot pick and choose which of God's love letters I will keep and which ones I will toss out. It is either ALL TRUE or none of it is. I either believe ALL OF IT or none of it. Scars in our lives can serve as catapults to launch us into the future God has planned and has been preparing us for as part of HIS PLAN, HIS WILL, and HIS STORY – this is our story and the purpose He has for our lives. These moments of our lives can prepare us and teach us how to authentically and whole-heartedly relate to God and to others.

PRAYER

Abba Father, help us to let go of our past. Help us to surrender past hurts, failures, regrets, and injuries done to us by others into Your trustworthy and reliable hands. Help us to trust You with these things Father. Give us courage. Help us to boldly step out. Help us to not hold grudges. Help us to not grow angry and bitter. Help us to pull up the deceitful roots of shame, regardless of their origin. Help us to let go of pain and guilt, and bewilderment. Father, today we surrender our lives. We pray you would bring a healing and cleansing rain. We pray you would breathe fresh air into our lungs. Help us Father to not be led by our emotions and faulty belief systems, but rather by Your truths that were ushered in to prepare the way long before the foundations of the earth were laid. Help us to grasp hold of Your beautiful love for us and believe it deep inside. Help us to reflect Your love and shine Your light on others. These mercies we ask in the mighty name of Jesus and in faith believing that You are not a man who can lie, but You are GOD who does not possess the ability to lie. You are true to Your nature. We love You and we thank You, Father, in Jesus' name, Amen and Amen. So, let it be done on earth as in Heaven.

Pour your heart out to God in the spaces provided below. Whatever comes to mind.

Daily release these tears from your heart to God and watch Him do what only He can do through a surrendered heart.

Thank you for allowing me to share my heart with you. May you find the courage to believe and hope. I promise you; it will be worth it.

_____

_____

_____

_____

_____

_____

_____

_____

_____

_____

_____

_____

ABOUT THE AUTHOR

VJ Goodman (Valerie) was born and raised in Shelby County, Alabama and now calls Southside, Alabama her home. She is the wife of a true ROCK STAR, and together she and Tommy parent four incredible adult kiddos, and are ViVi and Poppy to four beautiful granddaughters.

In June of 2019, Tommy and Valerie launched a local chapter of a national 501(c)(3) non-profit organization, serving children in need within a nine-county radius of their home. They attend Church of the Highlands, where they both serve in different capacities as members of the Dream Team.

Valerie has a rich and diverse history in ministry including non-profit marketing and development, past service as a worship leader in the local church, and leading small groups focused on equipping and encouraging women and families. She is passionate about furthering the Kingdom of God by allowing God to use what was intended to destroy to point others to the hope she found in Christ Jesus. Using her life experience, she strives to redefine what success is through her determination to overcome. She stands firm in her belief that we are made overcomers not only by the Blood of the Lamb, but also by the words of our testimonies.

Valerie's heart is that her story will first and foremost point people to Jesus. She recognizes that one of Satan's biggest tools in the arsenal is the one of isolation. Her heart is that women will discover beauty found in the context of connection with others, and a freedom that comes only from an authentic and vulnerable relationship with others and God. Helping others discover the foundational truth that *"God ISN'T SCARED of Our Ugly,"* is her mantra.

NOTES

1. *www.dictionary.com*
2. *onlinedictionary.com*
3. *Scriptures marked MSG are taken from The Message, copyright © 1993, 2002, 2018 by Eugene H. Peterson.*
4. *Great Balls of Fire by Jerry Lee Lewis, 1957 on Sun Records https://en.wikipedia.org/wiki/Great_Balls_of_Fire*
5. *Scriptures marked Holman Christian Standard Bible (HCSB) are taken from Holman Christian Standard Bible, Copyright © 1999, 2000, 2002, 2003, 2009 by Holman Bible Publishers, Nashville Tennessee. All rights reserved.*
6. *Scriptures marked NLT are taken from Holy Bible, New Living Translation, copyright © 1996, 2004, 2015 by Tyndale House Foundation. Used by permission of Tyndale House Publishers, Inc., Carol Stream, Illinois 60188. All rights reserved.*
7. *He's Still Working on Me by Joel Hemphill / The Hemphills, 1980, https://rateyourmusic.com/release/album/the-hemphills/workin-hes-still-working-on-me/*
8. *Scriptures marked NIV are taken from New International Version NIV, Holy Bible, New International Version®, NIV® Copyright ©1973, 1978, 1984, 2011 by Biblica, Inc.® Used by permission. All rights reserved worldwide.*
9. *Scriptures marked NCB are taken from Copyright © 2019 by Catholic Book Publishing Corp. All rights reserved.*
10. *Scriptures marked ESV are taken from The English Standard Version, The Holy Bible, English Standard Version. ESV® Text Edition: 2016. Copyright © 2001 by*

Crossway Bibles, a publishing ministry of Good News Publishers.
11. Dr. Joel Hoomans, March 20, 2015, Article: 35,000 Decisions: The Great Choices of Strategic Leaders https://go.roberts.edu/leadingedge/the-great-choices-of-strategic-leaders
12. https://www.craiggroeschel.com/
13. https://lysaterkeurst.com/
https://lysaterkeurst.com/category/boundaries/
14. Scriptures marked NASB are taken from New American Standard Bible®, Copyright © 1960, 1971, 1977, 1995, 2020 by The Lockman Foundation. All rights reserved.
15. https://lisaharper.org/store LIFE An Obsessively Grateful, Undone by Jesus, Genuinely Happy, and Not Faking Through the Hard Stuff Kind of 100-Day Devotional
16. https://easterbrothers.com/ Thank You Lord for Your Blessings on Me by the Easter Brothers, 1975
17. www.integratedlistening.com, definition of trauma
18. Scriptures marked MEV are taken from The Holy Bible, Modern English Version. Copyright © 2014 by Military Bible Association. Published and distributed by Charisma House.
19. Scriptures marked AMP are taken from Copyright © 2015 by The Lockman Foundation, La Habra, CA 90631. All rights reserved.

www.ingramcontent.com/pod-product-compliance
Lightning Source LLC
Chambersburg PA
CBHW031312160426
43196CB00007B/504